Volume **12** **THE**
GOLDEN BOOK
ENCYCLOPEDIA

mineral to Nevada

min-nev

An exciting, up-to-date encyclopedia
in 20 fact-filled, entertaining volumes

Especially designed as
a first encyclopedia for
today's grade-school children

More than 2,500 full-color
photographs and illustrations

GOLDEN ®

From the Publishers of Golden® Books

Western Publishing Company, Inc.
Racine, Wisconsin 53404

ILLUSTRATION CREDITS
(t=top, b=bottom, c=center, l=left, r=right)

1 l, Marie DeJohn/Publishers' Graphics; 1 r, Fiona Reid/Melissa Turk & The Artist Network; 5, Kenneth Garrett/Woodfin Camp; 6 tl, Phillip Hayson/ Photo Researchers; 6 b, Tom Powers/Joseph, Mindlin & Mulvey Inc.; 8, Van Bucher/Photo Researchers; 9 cr, Marilyn Bass; 10–11 t, Tom Powers/ Joseph, Mindlin & Mulvey Inc.; 11 br, U.S. Army; 12, Bettmann Archive; 13, Gary Lippincott/Publishers' Graphics; 15 tl, A. Keler/Sygma; 15 br, Marilyn Bass; 19 tl, Marilyn Bass; 19 br, Ron Sherman/Bruce Coleman Inc.; 20, David Lindroth Inc.; 21 br and 22 bl, Dennis O'Brien/Joseph, Mindlin & Mulvey Inc.; 22 tr, SPL/Photo Researchers; 23 photo, Tom McHugh/Steinhart Aquarium/Photo Researchers; 24 bl, Marc & Evelyne Bernheim/Woodfin Camp; 24 br, David Burnett/Woodfin Camp; 25 tr, Sandy Rabinowitz/Publishers' Graphics; 25 cr, Courtesy Museum of the American Indian, Heye Foundation; 25 br, George A. Gabriel; 26 tr and 27 tl, Sandy Rabinowitz/Publishers' Graphics; 27 br, Frank Mayo; 28 tr, Leonard Lee Rue III/Photo Researchers; 28 bl, Kenneth W. Fink/Bruce Coleman Inc.; 29, Alex Webb/Magnum; 31 tr, Marilyn Bass; 31 cl, © Joe Viesti; 32, Historical Pictures Service, Chicago; 33 b, Don Carl Steffen/Photo Researchers; 34 bl, Corporative Affairs Service, City of Montreal; 34–35 t, and 36–37 all, NASA; 38 b, W.E. Ruth/Bruce Coleman Inc.; 38 inset, J. Wright/Bruce Coleman Inc.; 39, Porterfield-Chickering/Photo Researchers; 40 cl, V. Englebert/Photo Researchers; 40 br, David Lindroth Inc.; 41 br, Scala/Art Resource; 42, Karel A. De Gendre/ANA/Viesti Associates; 43, Musée Condé, Chantilly/Giraudon/Art Resource; 44 t, Grandma Moses: *Sugaring Off*, Copyright © 1984, Grandma Moses Properties Co., New York; 45 bl, Virginia P. Weinland/Photo Researchers; 45 br, Gregory G. Dimijian, M.D./Photo Researchers; 46 tl, Copyright © 1916, 1944 Checkerboard Press, a Division of Macmillan, Inc., used by permission; 46 cr, Frank Mayo; 47 bl, Bettmann Archive; 47 br, Robert Frank/Melissa Turk & The Artist Network; 48, Dennis O'Brien/Joseph, Mindlin & Mulvey Inc.; 49 bl, Jacques Jangoux/Peter Arnold Inc.; 49 br, E.R. Degginger/Bruce Coleman Inc.; 50 tl, Nicholas deVore/Bruce Coleman Inc.; 51 both, Keith Gunnar/Bruce Coleman Inc.; 52 tr, Fiona Reid/Melissa Turk & The Artist Network; 52 bl, Wendell Metzen/Bruce Coleman Inc.; 53, Copyright 1988, Lucasfilm Limited, all rights reserved; 54 and 55 t, Richard Hutchings; 55 br, Richard Hutchings/Photo Researchers; 56, Culver Pictures; 58 tl, Robert Azzi/Woodfin Camp; 58 c, 95.1407a, Mummy of Nesmutaatneru, Egyptian, dynasty 25 or 26, H:151 cm, gift of Egypt Exploration Fund, courtesy Museum of Fine Arts, Boston; 59 and 60, Robert Frank/Melissa Turk & The Artist Network; 61 tl, Richard Hutchings; 61 bl, Ontario Science Centre; 61 br, Robert E. Murowchick/Photo Researchers; 62, Circus World Museum; 63 br, Stephen P. Parker/Photo Researchers; 63 inset, Tom Branch/Photo Researchers; 64 tl, Richard Hutchings; 65 bl, Lawrence Migdale/Photo Researchers; 65 br, Richard Hutchings; 66, Lowell Georgia/Photo Researchers; 67, Kathie Kelleher/Publishers' Graphics; 68–70 all, Marie DeJohn/ Publishers' Graphics; 71 and 72, Kathie Kelleher/Publishers' Graphics; 73 and 74, David Lindroth Inc.; 76 and 77 tl, Historical Pictures Service, Chicago; 78 and 80, Gary Lippincott/Publishers' Graphics; 81, Sandy Rabinowitz/Publishers' Graphics; 82, Dwight D. Eisenhower Library; 83 br, Art Resource; 84, Bettmann Archive; 85 tr, National Park Service; 85 bl, © Joe Viesti; 85 br, National Park Service; 86, Dick Durrance/Woodfin Camp; 87 bl, Lowell Georgia/Photo Researchers; 87 br, Philip Jon Bailey/Taurus Photos; 89 tr, Marilyn Bass; 89 bl, Francois Gohier/Photo Researchers; 90 tr, Charles F. Capen/Hansen Planetarium; 90 cr, David Lindroth Inc.; 91, Robert Frank/Melissa Turk & The Artist Network; 92, Biophoto Associates/Photo Researchers; 93 cl, Adam Woolfitt/Woodfin Camp; 95 bl, Arthur Sirdofksy; 95 br, Marilyn Bass; 96 bl, Craig Aurness/ Woodfin Camp.

COVER CREDITS
Center: NASA. Clockwise from top: SPL/Photo Researchers; Marie DeJohn/Publishers' Graphics; Tom Branch/Photo Researchers; Robert Frank/ Melissa Turk & The Artist Network; Kenneth W. Fink/Bruce Coleman Inc.; Lowell Georgia/Photo Researchers.

Library of Congress Catalog Card Number: 87-82741
ISBN: 0-307-70112-3

ABCDEFGHIJKLM

mineral

Minerals are among the most useful substances known to man. From some, we get the metals we need to build cars, airplanes, and bridges. Other minerals are used by farmers to fertilize crops. Still others provide us with the many chemical compounds needed in medicine and in manufacturing. To stay healthy, we must have certain minerals, such as selenium and copper, in our diets. We mine the earth for minerals such as gypsum, sulfur, and gold.

Minerals in Geology Some people call every material that comes from the earth a mineral. But the word has a special meaning to a *geologist*—a scientist who studies earth history, especially rocks—or to a *mineralogist*—a scientist who studies minerals. In geology, a substance must meet four requirements to be called a mineral.

First, the substance is found in nature. It is not made by people.

Second, it is *inorganic*. It is not formed by living things or by things that once lived. According to this rule, oil and coal would not be minerals, because they come from plant material.

Third, the chemical makeup of a substance is the same all over the world. Sand is not a mineral, because its chemical composition varies. Some minerals are made of atoms of a single element. These minerals are called *native elements* and include gold, silver, copper, and sulfur. Most minerals are formed of atoms of different elements. The mineral that we call *salt* and geologists call

halite, for example, is always made of atoms from two elements—sodium and chlorine. (*See* **element** and **compound.**)

Fourth, atoms in the substance form a specific pattern. This pattern is always a crystal. (*See* **crystal.**)

Scientists have discovered over 3,000 kinds of minerals and keep finding new ones. Nature has provided us with a vast storehouse of minerals in the rocks of the earth's crust. Some rocks consist of just one mineral. The rock quartzite is made of the mineral quartz, and limestone is made of calcium carbonate. Most rocks are made up of a variety of minerals. Granite contains the minerals quartz, mica, and feldspar. (*See* **granite** and **limestone.**)

Recognizing Minerals Minerals are easier to see in some kinds of rock than in others. For example, you can see the minerals in granite, which has cooled slowly underground, without a magnifying glass. But to see any of the minerals in cooled lava, you would need to use a microscope. Lava cools into solid rock very quickly, leaving mineral grains too small to see with the naked eye.

People have come up with tests that help them identify different minerals. Just looking at a mineral's color is not always a good guide. Tiny amounts of another element in a mineral can change its color completely. That is why quartz may appear white, gray, black, pink, lavender, green, or colorless.

Granite is a kind of rock made of several different minerals.

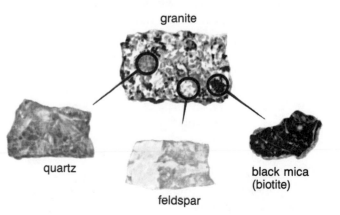

granite

quartz

feldspar

black mica (biotite)

KINDS OF MINERALS

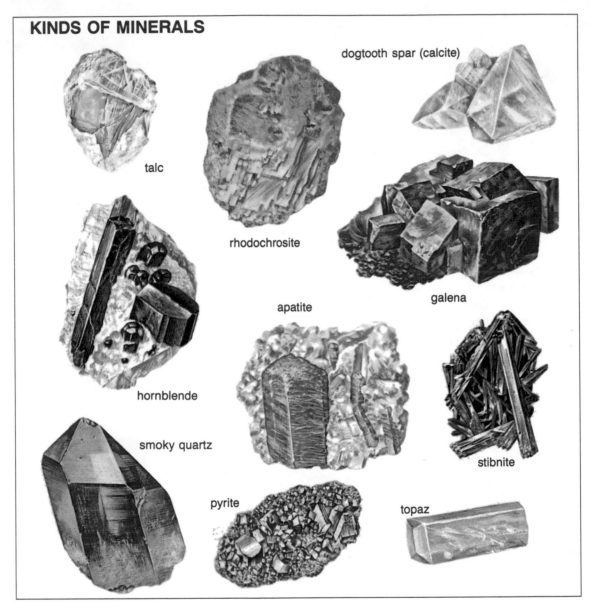

dogtooth spar (calcite)

talc

rhodochrosite

galena

hornblende

apatite

smoky quartz

stibnite

pyrite

topaz

The *streak test* is a better test for color. Rub the mineral on a white, rough surface. The mark left behind will show the mineral's color without impurities.

The mineral's *luster*—how it shines—can also help identify the mineral. Some minerals, such as gold, shine like metals. Talc looks pearly, and quartz looks glassy.

Hardness is another test. The hardness of a mineral is compared to the *Mohs scale*—a list of ten minerals. On this scale, talc is the softest mineral. You can scratch it with your fingernail. Diamond is the hardest—it can scratch all other materials.

How a mineral *breaks* is another test. Scientists look at the number of breaks and their directions. Mica, for example, always breaks into thin, flat sheets.

Crystals Each mineral has its own crystal shape. The shape is a clue to how the atoms in the crystal are arranged. A crystal of beryl, for example, has six sides because its atoms join together in a six-sided ring. Quartz crystals, too, have six sides. But the ends of quartz crystals are shaped like pyramids, while beryl crystals are flat. The sulfur and iron atoms of the mineral pyrite form crystals shaped like cubes. Another mineral with cube-shaped crystals is galena, which is made of sulfur and lead atoms. When scientists are not sure what kind of mineral they have, they x-ray it to see how the atoms are arranged.

How Minerals Form Minerals form in several ways. The minerals in granite begin to form from *magma*—hot, melted rock deep below the surface of the earth. Gases in the magma force it to flow upward through cracks in the earth's *crust*—its outer "skin." There the magma begins to cool.

When magma starts to cool, the atoms of its different elements begin to combine. An atom of iron, for example, will combine with two atoms of sulfur to form the mineral pyrite. When enough atoms of iron and sulfur have combined, a small crystal of pyrite appears. The crystal grows in size as long as there are atoms of iron and sulfur in the magma that are free to join it.

Granite forms from magma that cools very slowly, giving the atoms enough time to join together in orderly arrangements. When magma rises from a volcano and pours onto the earth's surface, it may cool off before the atoms can arrange themselves. When this happens, natural glass forms, instead of crystals. The most common form of volcanic natural glass is called *obsidian*.

Minerals also form on the earth's surface by the evaporation of seawater. This water has chemicals called *salts* dissolved in it. As the water evaporates, the molecules of these chemicals join to form crystals. The most familiar of these salt crystals is the table salt we use on food.

See also **geology; atom;** and **molecule.** See the Index for entries on individual minerals.

---

mining

The earth is full of valuable and useful materials—such as uranium, iron, quartz, gold, coal, diamonds. They are part of the rock and soil that make up our planet. Mining is the process of getting these materials from the earth.

About 8,000 years ago, prehistoric people learned that a kind of rock called *flint* could be made into sharp weapons and tools. Later, they discovered that striking metal against flint produced a spark for starting a fire. They began digging into the earth to collect flint. This was the beginning of mining.

The Bronze Age began when people started making tools from bronze—a mixture of copper and tin. People dug into the earth for *ore*—rock rich in a metal. An ancient copper mine, from around 4000 B.C., has been found in Israel. Around 1500 B.C., people learned how to use iron to make even stronger tools and weapons. During the Iron Age, people collected iron ore. Today, there are three main kinds of mining.

Placer Mining Placer mining is used to collect ore that is close to the earth's surface. The ore is usually in or along streams and

This giant machine is used in strip mining. It cuts deeply into the earth.

**This open-pit iron mine is
in western Australia.**

Panning for gold is an example of placer mining. When gold miners collect gold from a stream, they use a shallow pan to catch the sand and gravel being carried along by the water. Bits of gold are mixed in with the sand and gravel. Swirling the water in the pan washes away the sand and gravel, and leaves the heavier gold in the pan.

Dredging is similar to panning. In dredging, layers of soil, sand, and gravel are dug up from the bottoms of streams and rivers. Water is run through the mud to wash away the lighter materials and leave the heavy ores.

Hydraulic mining is another kind of placer mining. Powerful jets of water are shot at a hill or bank of gravel and loose rock. The force of the water washes away the light stone and leaves the heavy metal ore.

Open-Pit Mining In many areas of the world, deposits of coal, diamonds, and ores lie just under the topsoil. These can be reached by *open-pit mining* or by *strip mining*. In open-pit mining, bulldozers, steam

rivers. Placer mining requires no deep digging, because nature has already done much of the work. Glaciers, wind, and water have brought the ores to the surface.

**Coal miners use elevators to get down into the mine and to carry coal to the surface.
The mining is done in nearly level tunnels that meet the main shaft.**

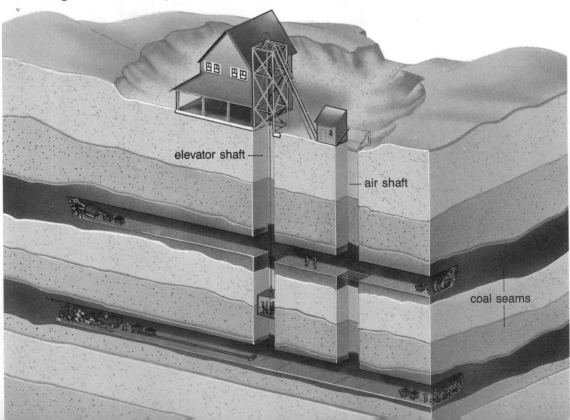

elevator shaft

air shaft

coal seams

shovels, and explosives dig a large, shallow *pit*—hole—in the earth. They dig the pit in stepped layers called *benches.* Roads or railroad tracks run along the benches so trucks or railroad cars can carry the ore out of the pit. In strip mining, bulldozers and steam shovels scrape away the soil to collect ores, minerals, or coal that lie just beneath the surface.

Both mining methods can be harmful to the environment. After the valuable deposits have been removed, ugly gashes are left in the land. These abandoned strip mines cause water pollution. Rainwater carries leftover minerals and metals from the mine into the underground water supply. Filling these mines with soil prevents such water pollution and lets people use the land again for other purposes.

Deep-Shaft Mines Reaching deposits deep in the earth requires the digging of *shafts*—tunnels that go straight down. Deep-shaft mines reach more than 1 mile (1.6 kilometers) underground. When a deposit is found, miners use machinery and explosives to dig horizontal tunnels into the deposit. These tunnels extend out like passages in underground cities. They go as far as necessary to get the entire deposit of gold, coal, or other material.

Another kind of deep-shaft mining is used to remove, salt, sulfur, and other minerals that dissolve or melt in water. Extremely hot water and steam are pumped down into the shaft. When they are pumped out of the shaft, they contain the minerals.

The most dangerous kind of deep-shaft mining requires people to work deep inside the earth. The air in a mine is full of dust that is harmful to the lungs. There are also poisonous gases underground. The gases and dust can explode easily. Just a spark from a machine can set off a tremendous gas or dust explosion. A powerful explosion can cause tunnels to cave in. Hundreds of miners are killed every year in such cave-ins.

In the United States and many other countries, safety laws require that the air in deep-shaft mines be made safe to breathe. Tunnels must be properly supported to help prevent cave-ins. Machines now do much of the underground work. But people are still needed for mining deep underground.

Today, scientists are looking under the ocean floor and in outer space for new sources of valuable materials. Satellites and high-flying aircraft have special instruments that can look at the earth and "see" where there are deposits of metals, minerals, and coal. Computers are used to study the satellite and aircraft pictures. They can discover deposits miles below the earth's surface and beneath the ocean floor.

Minneapolis

Minneapolis is the largest city in the state of Minnesota. It is on the Mississippi River and is an important center of trade, industry, and transportation. More than 2 million people live in or around Minneapolis and its "twin city." St. Paul is Minnesota's capital and second-largest city.

In 1680, the explorer Louis Hennepin discovered the Falls of St. Anthony on the Mississippi. The falls were important to the growth of Minneapolis. They provided waterpower for the city's two major industries—lumbering and flour milling. Today, the manufacture of farm equipment and computers is also important.

Minneapolis is nicknamed the "City of Lakes" because it has 22 lakes. The city is also known for its cold winters. Covered walkways have been built to connect many big buildings, so people do not have to go out in the cold.

Minneapolis has fine museums, including the Walker Art Center and the Minneapolis Institute of Arts. The Guthrie Theater is one of the nation's most famous theaters. Minneapolis and St. Paul have many colleges, including the giant University of Minnesota. There are many parks. In Minnehaha Park, Henry Wadsworth Longfellow wrote his famous poem *The Song of Hiawatha.*

Minnesota

Capital: St. Paul
Area: 84,402 square miles   (218,601 square kilometers)   (12th-largest state)
Population (1980): 4,075,970   (1985): about 4,193,000   (21st-largest state)
Became a state: May 11, 1858   (32nd state)

Have you read the *Little House* books by Laura Ingalls Wilder? They tell about pioneer children growing up in the Midwest in the late 1800s. *On the Banks of Plum Creek* is about a family settling in Minnesota to start a wheat farm. Laura Ingalls Wilder lived for a while in Walnut Grove, Minnesota.

Minnesota is a state in the north-central United States. If you put your finger right in the middle of a map of North America, you will touch Minnesota.

Minnesota is bordered by Canada on the north, Iowa on the south, Wisconsin and Lake Superior on the east, and North Dakota and South Dakota on the west. The state also includes the "Northwest Angle," a small piece of land north of Lake of the Woods. That land was supposed to be in Canada, but the mapmakers made a mistake! The Northwest Angle makes Minnesota the northernmost state, except for Alaska.

Land Most of the state was covered by *glaciers*—giant ice sheets—thousands of years ago. When the glaciers melted, they left behind many lakes, as well as hills and ridges. That is why Minnesota is nicknamed the "Land of 10,000 Lakes."

Minnesota's rivers flow in one of three directions. They go north to Hudson Bay, east to the Great Lakes, or south to the Gulf of Mexico. The longest river in the United States—the Mississippi—begins in Lake Itasca. (*See* **Mississippi River.**)

8

Eastern Minnesota receives about 30 inches (761 millimeters) of rain every year. Western Minnesota receives 20 to 24 inches (508 to 609 millimeters) a year.

Minnesota is rich in natural resources. It has huge forests, parts of which can be reached only by canoe. The forests are home to fur-bearing animals and provide timber, both important to the state's economy. More than half of the nation's iron ore comes from just a small section of Minnesota. The state has huge amounts of fertile farmland. The corn, hay, and oats raised there are used mostly as feed for animals. More turkeys are raised in Minnesota than in any other state. Minnesota's many dairy farms make it a leading producer of butter.

History Skeletons found in Minnesota show that people lived there 12,000 years ago. When white men arrived, Chippewa Indians lived in the forests, and the Sioux lived on the prairies. When the Indians were pushed off their lands, they fought back. One of the bloodiest Indian wars in history was the Sioux uprising of 1862.

People The first white settlers came from the eastern United States to Minnesota to farm. Most of these settlers came originally from Europe, particularly Germany, Finland, and the Scandinavian countries—Denmark, Norway, and Sweden. About half of all Minnesotans are descended from Scandinavians. Germans make up almost a quarter of the population. More than 11,000 Chippewa Indians live in Minnesota, mostly on *reservations*—areas set aside for Indians.

In below-zero cold, a sculptor carves an ice figure at the St. Paul Winter Carnival.

CANADA

Lake of the Woods

Rainy River

International Falls

Rainy Lake

Grand Portage

IMPORTANT FUR-TRADING POST OF THE 1700s

Upper Red Lake

Lower Red Lake

Lake Winnibigoshish

MESABI AND VERMILION RANGES (world's largest known deposits of iron ore).

Virginia

Hibbing

Silver Bay

Lake Superior

ELEVATION   Feet

2000 — 3000
1500 — 2000
1000 — 1500
600 — 1000

0   MILES   50

Bemidji

Lake Itasca

SOURCE OF THE MISSISSIPPI RIVER

Leech Lake

Mississippi River

Duluth

WISCONSIN

Moorhead

Red River of the North

NORTH DAKOTA

Fergus Falls

Brainerd

Mille Lacs Lake

BOYHOOD HOME OF CHARLES LINDBERGH

Little Falls

M I N N E S O T A

St. Croix River

▲ Historical Sites and Points of Interest

St. Cloud

Coon Rapids

UNIVERSITY OF MINNESOTA

Minneapolis ★ St. Paul

St. Louis Park

South St. Paul

Minnesota River

SOUTH DAKOTA

Pipestone

New Ulm

Faribault

Mankato

Owatonna

Worthington   Fairmont

Albert Lea   Austin

Red Wing

Winona

Rochester HOME OF THE MAYO CLINIC

IOWA

Pink and white lady's slipper

Common loon

Half of the state's people live in or around the Twin Cities—Minneapolis and St. Paul. Minneapolis is the largest city in the state. St. Paul is the state's capital and second-largest city. St. Paul is an important business, industrial, and transportation center. It is also the nation's biggest publisher of calendars and lawbooks. (*See* **Minneapolis.**)

Duluth is on Lake Superior. It is the third-largest city in Minnesota and has the nation's largest inland harbor. Iron ore, grain, crude oil, and many other items are shipped in and out of Duluth.

Tourism is an important part of Minnesota's economy today. Millions of visitors come to Minnesota each year to enjoy fishing, hunting, water sports, and winter sports, such as ice skating and skiing. Minnesota gives out more fishing licenses than any other state. It also has more boats per person than any other state.

Famous Minnesotans include former vice presidents Hubert H. Humphrey and Walter F. Mondale. The writers F. Scott Fitzgerald and Sinclair Lewis were from Minnesota, as is "Peanuts" cartoonist Charles Schulz.

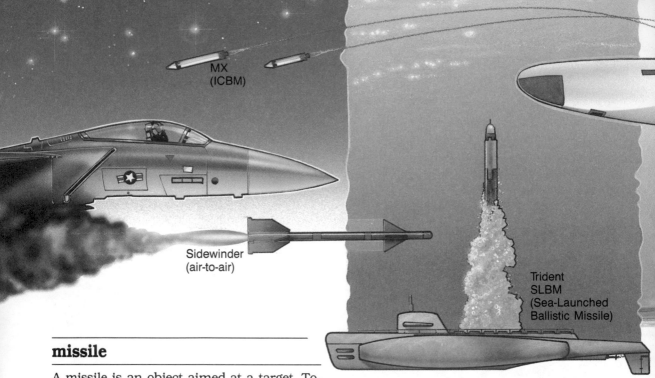

MX
(ICBM)

Sidewinder
(air-to-air)

Trident
SLBM
(Sea-Launched
Ballistic Missile)

missile

A missile is an object aimed at a target. To-day, we usually use the word to mean a long, tube-shaped weapon with an engine in the back and a *warhead* in front. The warhead is the part that carries the explosive. The main difference between a missile and a bullet is that the bullet has no engine. The first long-range missiles used in war were developed by the Germans during World War II. The missiles were called the V-1 and V-2. They were used to attack London and other targets in the United Kingdom.

Kinds of Missiles There are many kinds of missiles in use today. A *guided missile* is one that is steered to its target by radio or radar. The V-1 was a guided missile. The best-known missiles of this type today are called *cruise missiles.*

A *ballistic missile* has an an arching path. It rises and then falls like a ball thrown into the air. It rises until its fuel runs out, then drops to its target. It is guided only while it is powered. The V-2 was a ballistic missile.

One way to classify missiles is by their *range*—the distance they can travel. The missiles with the longest range are called *intercontinental ballistic missiles* (ICBMs). They can go thousands of miles to targets on the other side of the world. *Intermediate-range ballistic missiles* can travel up to about 1,800 miles (2,900 kilometers). Of all

Missiles can be shot from land, sea, or air. Some can travel halfway around the world.

ballistic missiles, *medium-range ballistic missiles* have the shortest range—up to 1,000 miles (1,600 kilometers). *Short-range missiles* are usually guided missiles.

Another way to classify missiles is by their launch sites—the places where they start their journeys—and by their targets. Some missiles can be launched only from the ground. Others can be launched from ships. Some missiles are fired from airplanes, and others from submarines. Missiles launched from the ground (or from ships) at targets that are also on the ground are called *surface-to-surface missiles*. Missiles launched from the ground (or from ships) at targets in the air are called *surface-to-air missiles*. Some airplanes carry missiles that can be fired from the air at other flying airplanes. These are called *air-to-air missiles*. Missiles fired from airplanes at targets on the ground are called *air-to-surface missiles*.

Some missiles, such as the Polaris missile, can be launched from underwater submarines. These missiles can be aimed at ground targets as far away as 4,000 to 5,000 miles (6,400 to 8,000 kilometers). Some submarines are also equipped to fire missiles at other submarines.

cruise missile
(radar-guided)

that fly very high, such as ballistic missiles, have rocket engines. At high altitudes, there is not enough oxygen to operate a jet engine. (*See* **jet engine** and **rocket**.)

Rocket engines can use liquid fuel or solid fuel. Liquid fuel is harder to store, so most modern missiles use solid fuel.

The explosive part of the missile—the warhead—may contain an ordinary explosive such as TNT, or a nuclear explosive. Some missiles can use either kind of explosive. Nuclear warheads are used mostly with ballistic missiles.

Since World War II, missiles have become very important weapons. They have also become more powerful and destructive. The United States and the Soviet Union have been trying to reach an agreement limiting the production of these dangerous weapons.

See also **nuclear weapon** and **weapon**.

How Missiles Are Guided There are several ways to guide a missile. One simple method is the *preset guidance system*. With this system, the missile's course, speed, and *altitude*—the height of its flight—are set before the missile is launched. All of the instructions for the flight are entered in an *automatic pilot*—a computer—in the missile. The automatic pilot keeps the missile on course to its target.

Another way of guiding a missile is to use a *beam rider system*. With this system, the missile follows a radar beam aimed at the target.

Many missiles are *homing missiles*. This means they have equipment that can detect heat or noise that is coming from the target. The missile then follows the heat or noise to the target. Many air-to-air missiles are "heat seekers." When fired at an enemy airplane, they follow the heat given off in the airplane's exhaust.

Some missiles have more than one guidance system. For example, a missile fired at an enemy bomber may be a beam rider until it gets close to the bomber, and then become a homing missile.

Engines and Warheads Missiles are powered by either a jet engine or a rocket engine. Both need oxygen to work. A jet engine gets oxygen from the atmosphere. A rocket engine carries its own supply. Missiles

With this shoulder-held missile launcher, a soldier can shoot an airplane.

mission

A mission is a settlement founded by members of a religious group for the purpose of teaching their religion to people who live nearby. Those who work to spread their religion in this way are called *missionaries.* (*See* **Christianity.**)

Beginning in the 1500s, Spanish missionaries came to the Americas hoping to spread Christianity to the Indians. Several United States cities, especially in the South and Southwest, were first settled as missions. Among them are Santa Fe, in New Mexico, and the California cities of San Francisco, Santa Barbara, and Monterrey.

Where Missions Started   Roman Catholic priests came from Spain to the Atlantic Coast of Florida in 1565. At St. Augustine, they built a mission that they called Nombre de Díos—which means "Name of God" in Spanish. This is the oldest mission in the United States. Parts of it still stand. The Spanish went on to found about 40 missions in Florida.

In the 1600s, Spanish missionaries moved north from Mexico into what is today New Mexico. In 1609, they founded the mission of

Flowers bloom in the courtyard of the mission in Carmel, California.

Santa Fe—"Holy Faith." Over the next few years, about 25 more missions were set up in New Mexico.

In the 1690s, the Spanish tried to establish missions in the area of present-day Texas. But Indians, including the Apache and Comanche, did not want the settlements on their land. They often attacked the missions and drove away settlers. Even so, a few missions did survive. One was the mission of San Antonio de Valero, founded in 1718. The mission later became the famous fort called the Alamo. The Battle of the Alamo was fought there in 1836, when Texas was trying to win its independence from Mexico. (*See* **Texas.**)

The most successful missions were those founded in California. In 1769, the Spanish priest Junípero Serra founded the mission of San Diego de Alcalá in southern California. Over the next 15 years, Serra built a string of missions along the Pacific coast. After Serra's death, others continued the work until there were 21 missions—from San Diego to San Francisco—"Saint Francis." A road called the *Camino Real*—"Royal Road"—connected the missions. Each was a day's ride on horseback from the next.

Mission Life   The Spanish missions were very much alike. Each had a church, where the missionaries and Indians worshipped daily. The church and several other buildings were clustered around a *plaza*—an open square. One building was usually a hospital, and another a school. Others were storehouses, craft workshops, dining rooms, and living areas for the missionaries. A few buildings were shelters for farm animals. Orchards and fields of grains and vegetables surrounded each mission. Nearby were small villages where the mission Indians lived.

Life in the missions followed a schedule of religious worship, schooling, and work. The priests gave clothing and food to the Indians. In return, the Indians agreed to study Christianity and to work on the mission. They constructed the buildings, cared for the

A California mission was like a small town. Indians lived nearby, and some worked inside the walls. The largest building inside the mission was the church (left).

animals, or worked the fields. Some Indians learned a craft in the mission's workshops. The missions often traded the goods produced in their shops.

During their stay at the missions, many Indians came to believe in Christian teachings and became Christians. Some Indians also accepted the Spanish way of life. They learned to speak Spanish, and they adopted Spanish customs. Many became farmers or ranchers. Others became blacksmiths, woodworkers, winemakers, and potters.

The End of the Spanish Missions Not all Indians accepted mission life. Many of them wanted to practice their own customs. They wanted to live as they always had. Often, Indians ran away from the missions. Spanish soldiers stood guard near the missions and forced the runaways to return. Many times, unhappy Indians attacked the missions, destroying buildings and crops.

The Spanish had hoped that the missions would attract settlers and increase the size of Spain's empire in the New World. But Spain went to war with France in the 1800s and lost control of many of its colonies in the Americas. Mexico took over the California missions in 1821. In 1834, the Mexican government began selling the rich lands owned by the missions. The Indians living at the missions were sent away and had to start new lives.

Today, most of the missions are in ruins. At some, the church and other buildings have been restored. They give clues to what mission life was like hundreds of years ago.

Mississippi

Capital: Jackson
Area: 47,689 square miles (123,515 square kilometers) (32nd-largest state)
Population (1980): 2,520,698 (1985): about 2,613,000 (31st-largest state)
Became a state: December 10, 1817 (20th state)

Mississippi is a state in the southern United States. Mississippi is bordered by Tennessee on the north, Alabama on the east, and Arkansas and Louisiana on the west. Its western border follows the great Mississippi River as closely as possible. In some places, the river has created horseshoe-shaped lakes called *oxbows*. So Mississipi's western border has wandered. Some towns built on the banks of the river were flooded. Others found that the river had moved away from them.

Land The whole state of Mississippi is a coastal lowland. Eastern and northeastern Mississippi are hilly. But even the biggest hill is only 806 feet (246 meters) high. The soil is rich in the northwestern part of the state. Soybeans and cotton are the chief crops there. Cattle are raised in the northeastern part of the state. Tree farms cover much of the coastal area.

Mississippi's climate is excellent for agriculture. Summers are hot, and winters are mild. Rainfall is abundant. In some places crops can grow all year long.

History In 1540, Spanish explorers entered the Mississippi region looking for gold and silver. They did not find the precious metals, but they did find Chickasaw, Choctaw, and Natchez Indians.

About 150 years later, the area was claimed by France. England won it away from France in 1763. Later in the 1700s,

Spanish troops controlled Mississippi. The United States did not gain control of the region until the early 1800s. This was long after the American Revolution and years after Mississippi had become a territory. All that time, Indians had fought to keep their land. By 1832, the last of the Indians had been moved west by the government.

Since the early 1800s, Mississippi farmers had been growing cotton. By the 1840s, large amounts of cotton were being grown in Mississippi and the rest of the South, on big farms called *plantations*. Plantation owners lived in large, beautiful houses with expensive furnishings. Black slaves did the work in the houses and fields. In Mississippi, black slaves made up more than half the population. In 1861, Mississippi joined the Confederate States of America and fought in the Civil War. Mississippi's leaders wanted to protect the state's economy and to keep slavery legal. (*See* **slavery; Confederate States of America;** and **Civil War.**)

Mississippi was ruined by the Civil War. Many people were killed or wounded, cities were destroyed, and the economy was wrecked. After the war, bad government made matters even worse. Mississippi was one of the poorest states in the nation until well into the 1900s.

Over the past few decades, Mississippi's economy has improved. Farmers have started using new methods, and the state has made great efforts to attract industry.

People Mississippi was settled by people from England, Ireland, and northern Europe. Their descendants make up almost two-thirds of the state's population. Almost all the rest are blacks, except for about 4,000 Choctaw Indians.

Most of the people still live on farms or in small towns. Mississippi's cities are growing as the state gets more industries, but none of the cities is very big yet. The biggest is Jackson, the capital. Jackson is a manufacturing center in the middle of the state.

One of Mississippi's most interesting cities is Vicksburg. It was an important port on

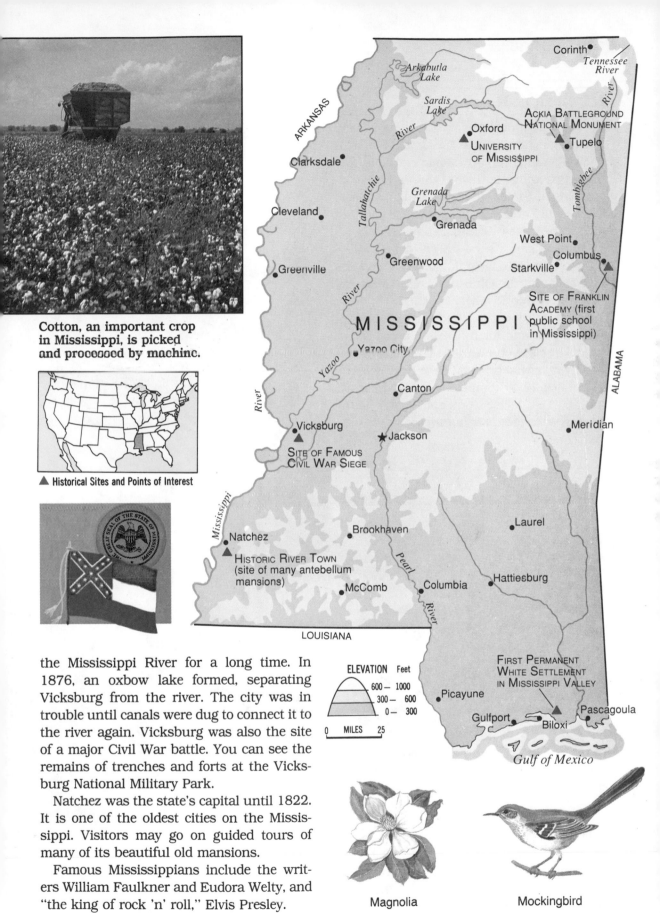

Cotton, an important crop in Mississippi, is picked and processed by machine.

▲ Historical Sites and Points of Interest

ARKANSAS

Corinth
Tennessee River

Arkabutla Lake

Sardis Lake

ACKIA BATTLEGROUND NATIONAL MONUMENT

Clarksdale

River

Oxford
▲ UNIVERSITY OF MISSISSIPPI

▲ Tupelo

Tallahatchie River

Grenada Lake

West Point

Cleveland

Grenada

Columbus ▲

Starkville

Greenville

Greenwood

SITE OF FRANKLIN ACADEMY (first public school in Mississippi)

Tombigbee River

M I S S I S S I P P I

Yazoo River

Yazoo City

Canton

Meridian

ALABAMA

River

Mississippi River

Vicksburg
▲ SITE OF FAMOUS CIVIL WAR SIEGE

★ Jackson

Laurel

Natchez
▲ HISTORIC RIVER TOWN (site of many antebellum mansions)

Brookhaven

Pearl River

McComb

Columbia

Hattiesburg

LOUISIANA

ELEVATION Feet

600 — 1000
300 — 600
0 — 300

0   MILES   25

FIRST PERMANENT WHITE SETTLEMENT IN MISSISSIPPI VALLEY ▲

Picayune

Pascagoula

Gulfport

Biloxi

Gulf of Mexico

the Mississippi River for a long time. In 1876, an oxbow lake formed, separating Vicksburg from the river. The city was in trouble until canals were dug to connect it to the river again. Vicksburg was also the site of a major Civil War battle. You can see the remains of trenches and forts at the Vicksburg National Military Park.

Natchez was the state's capital until 1822. It is one of the oldest cities on the Mississippi. Visitors may go on guided tours of many of its beautiful old mansions.

Famous Mississippians include the writers William Faulkner and Eudora Welty, and "the king of rock 'n' roll," Elvis Presley.

Magnolia

Mockingbird

Mississippi River

The Mississippi River is the longest and most important river in the United States. It is 2,348 miles (3,780 kilometers) long and flows generally southward through the central United States. It begins in Lake Itasca, Minnesota, and empties into the Gulf of Mexico near New Orleans, Louisiana.

Many other rivers—called *tributaries*—flow into the Mississippi. The largest are the Missouri and the Ohio rivers. (*See* **Missouri River** and **Ohio River**.)

South of the Ohio, the lower Mississippi twists back and forth across a broad *floodplain*—the area built up when soil is deposited by floodwater. Parts of the river here are 1½ miles (2.4 kilometers) wide. Near its mouth, the Mississippi splits into many branches, called *distributaries.*

Mississippi Riverboat

In the middle 1800s, hundreds of steamboats like these carried freight and passengers on the Mississippi.

From Wheels, Sails and Wings,
© C. Bertelsmann Verlag, 1959

The Mississippi carries a great deal of earth and sand, called *silt.* This silt builds up at the river's mouth, forming a *delta*—a broad, flat area of fertile land. The river brings so much silt that the delta is growing toward the sea at a rate of 6 miles (9.7 kilometers) every hundred years.

Much work has been done on the Mississippi to prevent the floods that were once common in the Mississippi basin, and to keep shipping channels open. High banks have been built along the sides of the river to hold the water in. Special channels called *spillways* carry extra water safely away. Dams across some of the tributaries control the amount of water that enters the Mississippi. The bottom of the river has been dug out to make it deeper and straighter.

The Mississippi River System is made up of the Mississippi plus its tributaries. If you count just the Mississippi and the Missouri, the system is 3,880 miles (6,247 kilometers) long. It is the third-longest river system in the world, after the Nile and the Amazon.

Water from 31 states and two Canadian provinces flows into the Mississippi River system. The Mississippi's drainage basin stretches from the northern Rocky Mountains eastward for more than 1,700 miles (2,737 kilometers) to the Appalachian Mountains. It forms one of the best agricultural regions in the world.

The Mississippi has always been used for transportation. The Indians knew how important it was—they named it "Great River" or "Father of Waters." Hernando de Soto, a Spanish explorer, was the first European to see the Mississippi. He crossed the lower part of the river in 1541. The French explorers Jacques Marquette and Louis Jolliet scouted the upper part in 1673. A few years later, Sieur de la Salle reached the mouth of the river. France then claimed the entire Mississippi basin. The French built a chain of fur-trading posts along the river. Then *plantations*—large farms—were established along the banks of the lower Mississippi. In 1803, the United States bought the land from France. (*See* **De Soto, Hernando; Marquette, Jacques; Jolliet, Louis; La Salle, Sieur de;** and **Louisiana Purchase.**)

Steamboats began traveling up and down the Mississippi in 1811. This made it much easier for planters near the river to ship their cotton, tobacco, and other crops to markets. Cities on the banks of the Mississippi began to grow rapidly.

Not all of the steamboats carried freight. Some were "showboats"—like floating theaters. During the Civil War, between 1861 and 1865, some carried armies and supplies.

After the Civil War, the United States was crossed east and west by railroads and canals. The Mississippi became less important as a north-south route for transportation. But after World War I ended in 1918, there was too much traffic on railroads and roads. The Mississippi became a major shipping route once again.

Barges loaded with cotton, sulfur, and petroleum move northward up the Mississippi. Sand, gravel, coal, and manufactured products move southward. Large ships can sail on the Mississippi, all the way from St. Paul, Minnesota, to the Gulf of Mexico. Tributaries and canals link the Mississippi with the Great Lakes and the St. Lawrence Seaway. The Intracoastal Waterway—a system of rivers, bays, and canals—connects it to cities as far away as Boston, Massachusetts. The Mississippi River has a special place in the hearts of Americans. Mark Twain and many others have written books and stories about life on the river.

Most of the rivers in the central United States (from the Rocky Mountains to the Appalachians) flow into the Mississippi.

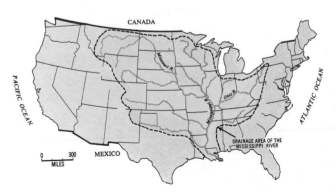

Missouri

Capital: Jefferson City
Area: 69,697 square miles (180,515 square kilometers) (18th-largest state)
Population (1980): 4,916,759 (1985): about 5,029,000 (15th-largest state)
Became a state: August 10, 1821 (24th state)

Missouri is a state in the central United States. Missouri's nickname is "Gateway to the West" because many people heading for the western states traveled on its rivers, trails, and highways. Its location and its two great rivers—the Mississippi and the Missouri—have made it a center of water, land, and air travel. Today, the giant Gateway Arch in St. Louis reminds people of the state's nickname. The people who stayed and settled in Missouri have made it an important farming and manufacturing state.

Land The Missouri River makes up part of the state's western border. At Kansas City, the Missouri turns east and flows through the middle of the state. It flows into the Mississippi River near St. Louis. The Mississippi River forms the state's eastern border. In the days before airplanes and cars, people used these rivers like highways. Rafts and steamboats carried people and freight up and down the rivers.

Two important trails to the West began in Independence. The Santa Fe Trail led to Spanish settlements in New Mexico. The Oregon Trail went to Oregon and California. Today, airports, railroads, and interstate highways connect Missouri with the West and East.

About half the land in Missouri is used for farming. The best farm land is in the northern half of the state. Important farm products include soybeans, corn, beef cattle, and hogs. Farmers in the southeastern corner of the state, sometimes called the "Bootheel," grow cotton.

The rest of the state is covered with forests and hills. The Ozark Mountains are in the southern part of the state. The Ozarks are not very high compared to other mountains, but they have many lakes, streams, and forests. People from Missouri and neighboring states enjoy vacationing in the Ozarks.

History Indians called Mound Builders lived in Missouri for centuries before Europeans arrived. When Europeans came, they met many tribes, including the Osage, Sauk, and Fox. The Missouri River got its name from the Missouri Indians, who lived near its mouth. The name is an Indian word that means "town of the big canoes."

In the 1600s, France claimed Missouri and other lands west of the Mississippi River. France gave the lands to Spain in the 1700s, but soon took them back. In 1803, France sold all its lands west of the Mississippi to the United States. (*See* **Louisiana Purchase.**)

In 1821, Missouri became the 24th state. But before Missouri could become a state, the Northern and Southern states quarreled bitterly over whether slavery would be permitted in Missouri. In 1820, the Missouri Compromise was passed. It allowed slavery in Missouri but outlawed it in Maine, which was becoming a state at the same time. When the Civil War started, Missouri was caught between North and South. Both sides hoped that Missouri would join them. In the end, Missouri stayed with the North, but many young men from Missouri joined the Southern armies. In some cases, brothers fought against each other. (*See* **Civil War.**)

After the war ended in 1865, the cities of Missouri began to grow. Thousands of German immigrants came to St. Louis, and it became an important manufacturing city. It could send goods to distant markets by riverboat or railroad. Today, St. Louis is Missouri's largest city. Its factories make cars, truck trailers, railroad and subway cars, and airplanes. Beer is another important product.

IOWA

NEBRASKA

Grand River

Chariton River

ILLINOIS

Kirksville

St. Joseph
▲ STARTING POINT FOR THE PONY EXPRESS

Chillicothe

Hannibal ▲
A CHILDHOOD HOME OF MARK TWAIN

Moberly

Kansas City

Independence
▲ HOME OF PRESIDENT HARRY TRUMAN
▲ EASTERN TERMINAL OF THE SANTA FE AND OREGON TRAILS

UNIVERSITY OF MISSOURI ▲
Columbia

Fulton

St. Charles

Sedalia

Mississippi

★ Jefferson City

St. Louis

MISSOURI

Missouri River

KANSAS

Osage River

Lake of the Ozarks

Meramec River

River

Rolla

Ste. Genevieve

Nevada

Lebanon

Lamar

O Z A R K

Joplin
▲ BIRTHPLACE OF GEORGE WASHINGTON CARVER

Carthage

Springfield

Cape Girardeau

P L A T E A U

OKLAHOMA

Table Rock Lake

Bull Shoals Lake

Ozark National Scenic Riverways ▲

Poplar Bluff

Sikeston

KENTUCKY

ARKANSAS

TENNESSEE

▲ Historical Sites and Points of Interest

Bluebird

Hawthorn

ELEVATION   Feet
1500 — 2000
1000 — 1500
 600 — 1000
 300 —   600
   0 —   300

0   MILES   50

The arch in St. Louis, on the western bank of the Mississippi River, is the gateway to the western United States.

On Missouri's western border, Kansas City became a market center for the ranches and farms of the Great Plains. Ranchers drove their herds of cattle to Kansas City, and meat-packing became an important business. Farmers shipped grain, which was ground into flour. Today, Kansas City provides a variety of manufactured goods as well as food products.

The capital of the state, Jefferson City, is on the Missouri River, about halfway between Kansas City and St. Louis. Other large cities include Springfield in the southwest and St. Joseph in the northwest.

Many famous Americans came from Missouri. Harry S. Truman was president of the United States from 1945 to 1953. Samuel Clemens—who took the pen name Mark Twain—grew up in the Mississippi River town of Hannibal. Scott Joplin was a black musician who helped create the music known as "ragtime." Joplin settled in Sedalia, Missouri, in the 1890s.

Missouri River

The Missouri is the second-longest river in the United States. It is 2,315 miles (3,727 kilometers) long and flows mostly southeastward through the north-central United States. Only the Mississippi is longer. (*See* **Mississippi River.**)

The Missouri begins where the Jefferson, Madison, and Gallatin rivers join, in the Rocky Mountains of Montana. The Missouri first flows north and then east through Montana. It turns southeast to cross North Dakota and South Dakota. The river continues along the boundaries between South Dakota and Nebraska, Iowa and Nebraska, and Missouri and Kansas. At Kansas City, Missouri, the Missouri turns east again and flows across the state of Missouri. It reaches the Mississippi River at Alton, Illinois, a few miles north of St. Louis, Missouri.

The Missouri has many *tributaries*—rivers that flow into it. The Missouri, in turn, is the longest tributary of the Mississippi River. Half of the Mississippi's water comes from the Missouri.

The Missouri drains about 529,400 square miles (1,371,146 square kilometers) of land. This area is called the Missouri River *basin*.

The Missouri is nicknamed "Big Muddy" because its waters carry a lot of soil. The mud used to build up into sandbars, making it difficult for boats to travel on the river. There were serious floods, with water levels sometimes rising more than 30 feet (9 meters). The Missouri River Basin Program, a government project that began in 1944, has helped to solve these problems. Under this program, many dams were built to control flooding, and a shipping lane is kept clear.

The river is named for the Missouri Indians, who lived at the river's mouth—the place where it empties into the Mississippi. French explorers Jacques Marquette and Louis Jolliet were the first Europeans to see the Missouri. They found the river's mouth in 1673, while exploring the Mississippi River. Then French fur traders began going up the Missouri. The Missouri River basin became part of the United States with the Louisiana Purchase in 1803. American explorers Meriwether Lewis and William Clark traveled the entire length of the river between 1804 and 1805. (*See* **Marquette, Jacques; Jolliet, Louis;** and **Lewis and Clark Expedition.**)

Traders and settlers used the river as a canoe "highway" into the Missouri River basin. Manufactured goods were sent in by canoe or shallow-bottomed boat. Furs, hides, and grains were shipped out.

During the 1800s, steamboats carried goods up and down the river. Many pioneers going west traveled by steamer on the Missouri. After railroads were built across the basin in the late 1800s, there was less traffic on the river. Today, the Missouri is again an important transportation route.

mold

Mold is a kind of fungus. Molds get their food from the materials they live on. They live on *organic* materials—living things, or things that once were alive. Molds often look like a cottony or powdery covering.

Molds form tiny threads called *hyphae*. The hyphae release chemicals that digest the food. Then the molds absorb the food and use it.

One common mold is black bread mold. It grows as a thin, black coating on moist

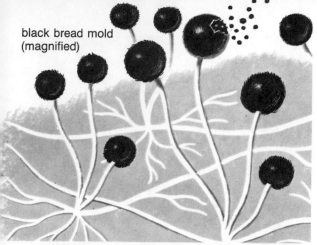

black bread mold
(magnified)

**Threadlike hyphae and the spore cases
in a magnified view of black bread mold.**

bread. Seen under a microscope, black bread mold looks like threads covering the surface of the bread. Some of the threads grow upright and have a knob on the top. Each knob is a *spore case* filled with millions of black *spores*. When the knob breaks open, the spores are carried in the air. The spores will develop into more black bread mold. These spores have been found all over the world. They are in the air over the North Pole and even over oceans far from land.

Many molds live in the soil. Some of them grow hyphae that have little loops in them. When tiny soil worms get trapped by the loops, the molds use the worms for food.

Some molds damage plants used for food. A gray mold that can grow on many kinds of berries and vegetables makes both the plants and the fruits rot. In Ireland in the 1840s, a mold destroyed almost the entire potato crop. A mold called *chestnut blight* has nearly wiped out the American chestnut tree. Today, many substances are used to protect food plants from destruction by molds.

Other molds grow on food after it is harvested. Often these molds produce poisonous or cancer-causing chemicals. Grains, beans, and peanuts are treated and inspected to keep these molds from causing harm.

Some molds are helpful to people. The most famous is *Penicillium,* the mold that is the source of the antibiotic penicillin. Molds also produce the flavor in some cheeses, such as Roquefort.

See also **fungus** and **penicillin.**

molecule

If you divided a drop of water into smaller and smaller parts, what is the very smallest part you could make and still have water? The smallest unit of water—and of most other substances—is one *molecule.*

What would happen if you tried to divide a single water molecule? There would be no water left. Molecules are made up of *atoms* —tiny building blocks of elements. A water molecule is made of two atoms of the element hydrogen and one atom of the element oxygen. A water molecule can be broken into these atoms, but then it is not water anymore. (*See* **atom.**)

The water molecule is quite simple. It is made of only three atoms. Some molecules are much more complicated. For example, a molecule of sugar has 45 atoms. A single molecule of dioxyribonucleic acid (DNA) has millions of atoms, yet there is DNA in nearly every cell in your body.

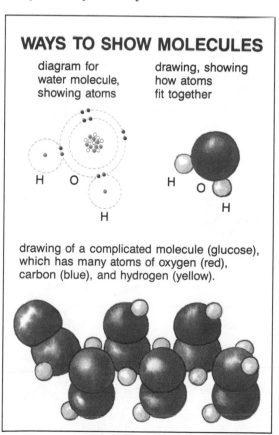

WAYS TO SHOW MOLECULES

diagram for
water molecule,
showing atoms

drawing, showing
how atoms
fit together

H   O

H

H   O

H

drawing of a complicated molecule (glucose),
which has many atoms of oxygen (red),
carbon (blue), and hydrogen (yellow).

The atoms in molecules are held together by forces in the different atoms. In some molecules, the forces between the atoms are very strong. These molecules are very difficult to break down into elements. The forces between the oxygen and hydrogen atoms in a water molecule are very strong. In other molecules, the forces between the atoms are weak. These molecules can be broken down into elements more easily.

There are also forces in molecules that attract other molecules of the same substance. In a solid, these forces between molecules are very strong. The molecules are "locked" into place among other molecules. They are always moving, but they can only *vibrate*—move back and forth very quickly over a small distance.

If the forces between the molecules are weaker, the substance may be a liquid. In a liquid, molecules can move more freely. If the forces between molecules are very weak, the substance will be a gas. Molecules in a gas can move about very freely.

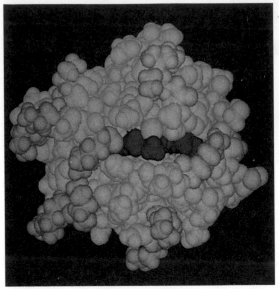

A computer graphic of a large protein molecule. Atoms of different elements are shown in different colors.

For a long time, scientists knew that there were molecules, but no one had ever seen one. After the electron microscope was invented in 1940, scientists were able to see molecules for the first time.

mollusk

Mollusks are *invertebrates*—animals without backbones. Most do not have internal skeletons. A mollusk can usually be recognized by the hard shell that surrounds its body. Clams, oysters, and snails are mollusks. Octopuses, squid, and slugs do not have hard shells, but they are mollusks, too. They are like their shelled relatives in some ways.

Mollusk comes from a Latin word meaning "soft." All mollusks have soft bodies. Around the body is a fold of tissue called the *mantle*. In mollusks with shells, the mantle builds the shell from lime—calcium carbonate. The mantle adds to the shell throughout the animal's life. How fast the shell grows depends on many factors—such as temperature, and the amount of lime available to the mollusk.

All mollusks have a muscular foot. This foot has different shapes and uses. The snail has a large foot, which it uses to creep along the ground. The clam, too, has a large foot, which it uses to dig. The octopus and squid

SOLID
Molecules in a solid (such as a spoon) are close together and vibrate in an orderly pattern.

LIQUID
Molecules in a liquid (such as milk) are farther apart and move more freely.

GAS
Molecules in a gas (such as natural gas) are very far apart and move very freely.

have feet that are divided into long tentacles, used for catching food.

Mollusks are found almost everywhere. Most kinds live in the sea. Some live in rivers and lakes. Others—such as many snails and slugs—live on land. There are about 100,000 known kinds of mollusks. The smallest are so tiny they are almost invisible. The largest is the giant squid, which may be more than 18 meters (60 feet) long.

Mollusks eat various foods. Some, such as oysters, are filter feeders. They get their nourishment by straining tiny bits of food out of the water. Other mollusks, such as land snails, eat plants. Still other mollusks,

such as octopuses, are carnivores—meateaters—that hunt other animals.

Mollusks are important to people. Snails, clams, scallops, squid, and other mollusks are popular foods. Oysters and freshwater mussels produce pearls. Many people collect mollusk shells, which are often very beautiful to look at.

Some mollusks are pests. For example, the shipworm is a clam that digs into wood. It causes damage to wooden ships, piers, and wharves. Some snails and slugs eat garden plants and do damage to crops.

See also **clams and mussels; octopuses and squid; oyster; pearl;** and **snail.**

KINDS OF MOLLUSKS

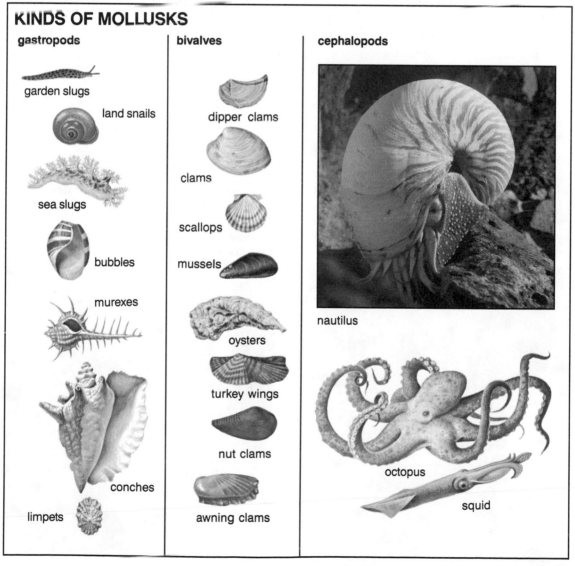

gastropods

garden slugs

land snails

sea slugs

bubbles

murexes

conches

limpets

bivalves

dipper clams

clams

scallops

mussels

oysters

turkey wings

nut clams

awning clams

cephalopods

nautilus

octopus

squid

Monaco, *see* Europe

monarchy

Monarchy is a form of government in which a monarch is the ruler. The monarch may be a king or queen, an emperor or empress, a prince or princess, or a sultan. A monarch rules as long as he or she lives. The position of monarch is usually inherited—passed from parent to child, most often from father to son. If there is no son, a daughter may inherit the throne. One of the greatest English monarchs, Elizabeth I, became queen after her brother died. (*See* **Elizabeth I.**)

In the past, monarchs had great power. People obeyed them because they believed the monarchs were given their powers by God. Church leaders crowned them and gave them symbols of authority, such as a golden *scepter*—rod. Monarchs sat on thrones that raised them above the rest of the people. They ate better than everyone else and wore much finer clothing.

Today, most monarchs have limited powers. They unite their people by serving as living reminders of their nations' history and traditions. England, Sweden, Denmark, the Netherlands, Belgium, Spain, Morocco, Jordan, Japan, and Nepal are countries with limited monarchies. On the other hand, the king of Oman, in the Middle East, has absolute—unlimited—power.

See also **kings and queens.**

monastery, *see* monks and monasteries

moneran

A moneran is a simple one-celled living thing. A moneran is not an animal, a plant, a protist, or a fungus, because it has no cell nucleus. Instead, a moneran has genetic material floating free inside it.

There are two large groups of monerans—bacteria and blue-green bacteria. The blue-green bacteria are sometimes known as *blue-green algae.*

Monerans live in the air, soil, and water. They also live in or on many other living things. They can live where it is very cold or very hot. A few monerans cause diseases in humans and other living things.

Monarchs dress in different ways. At left, an African king covers his face with a special mask. At right, Emperor Hirohito of Japan wears a business suit.

Blue-green bacteria contain chlorophyll and make their own food by photosynthesis. Bacteria cannot make their own food. They get food from living things and from living things that have died. Bacteria are important as *decomposers.* By eating dead animals and plants, they *decompose*—break down—the materials into elements. Plants then use those elements for growth.

Sometimes, blue-green algae in lakes and ponds divide and increase very rapidly. They form a mat on the water called a *bloom.* When this happens, the monerans use up their food and die. This can make a lake bad for swimming and boating.

See also **bacteria** and **cell.**

We can make trades for anything we find valuable. Early peoples used wampum and many other objects as money (below).

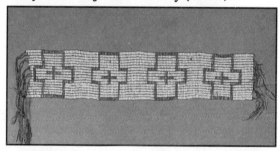

Chinese branch money

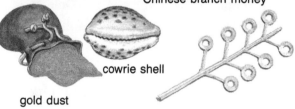

cowrie shell

gold dust

money

Imagine what it would be like if there were no such thing as money. Instead of buying things, you would trade for them. For example, you might get a new bicycle by giving its owner something in exchange. Before money was invented, this was the way people "bought" things. They traded something they had for something someone else had. This is called the *barter system.*

A problem with the barter system is that you can only trade with someone who wants what you have. Suppose the owner of the bicycle did not want what you had to trade. You would then need to find someone who had what the bicycle owner wanted. After you traded for that, you could trade for the bicycle.

Mediums of Exchange Trade is easier if there is a *medium of exchange*—something that everyone accepts in trade. It must be something that everyone thinks is valuable. Furs, gold, and silver are some of the things that have been used as mediums of exchange. Whales' teeth and cigarettes have also been used as mediums of exchange. Some American Indians used carved shells called *wampum* to buy and sell things.

All mediums of exchange have three things in common. First, people want them.

Second, they can be used over and over again. Third, they are easy to recognize.

In the United States and Canada, at one time, everyone would accept furs in trade for such items as food and clothing. Everyone considered furs valuable. They did not wear out quickly, and everyone knew what a fur looked like.

Metals make good mediums of exchange. Gold, silver, copper, bronze, nickel, and iron were made into *ingots*—bars. When used for buying something, a bar was weighed to find out how much it was worth. If the whole bar was not needed to pay for an item, some of the metal was cut or shaved from the bar.

Functions of Money For something to work as well as money does, it must do three things. First, it must serve as a medium of exchange. People must be willing to take it in exchange for such necessary things as food and clothing.

Second, it must serve as a way of measuring the value of things. For example, if one bicycle costs $100 and another bicycle costs $150, the second bicycle is worth more than the first one.

Third, money must serve as a "storehouse of value." This means that money earned today does not have to be spent immediately. You can save your money and spend it later. In the barter system, goods such as eggs could be stored for only a short time. When they spoiled, no one wanted them.

Today, most of the world uses a money system instead of bartering goods. The first kind of money was the coin.

Coins The earliest coins were used in a small country called Lydia (modern-day Turkey) in the 700s B.C. These coins were made from *electrum*—a mixture of gold and silver. The more electrum in a coin, the larger it was and the more value it had. Gold and silver had been used earlier as mediums of exchange, but not in the form of coins.

Coins were easier to use than ingots. Each coin had a certain size and value. Instead of weighing the coins, all you had to do was count them.

These early coins were a kind of *commodity money*. Commodity money has the same value as the material from which it is made. A dime containing 10 cents worth of silver would be an example of commodity money.

Since coins were counted, instead of weighed, some people cheated by shaving some of the metal off the edges. Shaving made the coins worth less. To prevent this, little grooves were put on the edges of the coins. These grooves are called *milling*. With *milled* edges, it is easy to tell if anyone has cut part of the metal off the coin. If you look at the edge of a dime or a quarter, you will see the milled edges.

Metals such as gold and silver have often served as money.

When settlers came to America, they brought the coins of their native countries with them. Coins from many countries were used in the colonies. One coin was the Spanish dollar. It was called a *piece of eight* because it was often chopped into eight pieces. The small pieces were called *bits*. In the United States, a quarter is still sometimes called "two bits."

The British allowed only the Massachusetts Bay Colony to make coins. The first coins made in the colonies were threepence, sixpence, and twelvepence pieces. A *pence* was a penny, so a threepence piece was worth 3 cents. These coins were made in 1652. The United States Mint now makes all the coins used in the United States. Congress established the United States Mint on April 2, 1792. The Canadian government makes all of Canada's coins.

Today's coins are not commodity money—the value of the metal they contain is not equal to the coins' value. This kind of money is called *fiat money*. A dime no longer contains 10 cents worth of silver, but it can still buy 10 cents worth of goods. Everyone will accept the dime as being worth 10 cents. Quarters, half-dollars, and "silver" dollars also are not made of silver anymore. They are made of nickel and copper. (*See* **coin.**)

Paper Money Most of the money in the United States today is paper money. It is easier to carry and to use than coins.

With a check or credit card, people can buy and sell without any coins or bills.

Before the Civil War in the 1860s, paper money in the United States was printed by individual banks. This paper money was in the form of *bank notes.* A bank note is a written promise from the bank to pay the amount stated on the bank note. The bank was supposed to pay gold or silver to anyone who had a bank note. This system did not work very well because many banks printed too many notes. They did not have enough gold or silver to back up their notes.

During the Civil War, the federal government started printing paper money to pay for the war. This money was green on one side, just as it is today. That is why paper dollars are sometimes called "greenbacks." From that time on, only the federal government could issue money.

The United States used to be on the *gold standard.* This means that you could trade your paper money for gold. If you had a $10 bill, you could take it to a bank and get $10 worth of gold. Money that can be taken to a bank and traded in for something valuable, like gold or silver, is called *credit money* or *fiduciary money.*

The United States went off the gold standard in 1933. Today, you cannot trade your paper money in for anything except coins or other paper money. In other words, the paper money that is now being used in the United States—*Federal Reserve notes*—is fiat money.

Checking Accounts Paper money and coins are known as *currency* or *cash.* Today, many people use checks instead of cash, especially if they are paying bills or ordering goods by mail. The money deposited in a checking account is called a *demand deposit.* This money can be taken out of the bank any time the depositor asks for it—that is, upon demand. The two kinds of money that are most commonly used in the United States are currency and demand deposits. (*See* **bank.**)

WHO IS ON THE MONEY

Most U.S. bills and coins show presidents, but Susan B. Anthony is on the silver dollar and Benjamin Franklin is on the $100 bill.

Lincoln penny

Jefferson nickel

Roosevelt dime

Washington quarter

Kennedy half-dollar

Susan B. Anthony silver dollar

Mongolia, *see* Asia

monkey

A monkey is a mammal that is closely related to humans and apes. There are 130 different kinds. The smallest monkeys, marmosets, may weigh less than 1 kilogram (2¼ pounds). Baboons, the largest monkeys, may weigh as much as 70 kilograms (150 pounds).

Most monkeys live in forests and spend much of their time in trees. Their strong legs, feet, arms, and hands help them climb and leap from tree to tree. The tips of the toes and fingers have pads covered with ridges, which help prevent slipping and skidding. Most monkeys have long tails that they use for balancing. Some monkeys can grasp branches and other objects with their tails as well as with their hands and feet.

Monkeys feed mainly on leaves, flowers, and fruits. They will also eat insects, small animals, and eggs. They eat in much the same way people do, picking up the food and carrying it to their mouths. Some monkeys

The mandrill is an Old World monkey with a colorful face and "beard."

A spider monkey is a New World monkey. It can grasp branches with its tail.

have pouches in their cheeks. They stuff food into these pouches, then remove the food when they have more time to chew.

Mother monkeys usually have one baby at a time. The baby is very dependent on its mother. The mother nurses it, keeps it warm, and protects it from enemies. A youngster may stay with its mother for several years before going off on its own. Monkeys may live to be 20 or 30 years old.

Scientists classify all monkeys in one of two groups—Old World and New World. Old World monkeys are native to Asia and Africa. They have rounded noses, and their nostrils are close together. Some Old World monkeys are active during the day and sleep at night. Others are active at night and sleep all day long. Old World monkeys cannot hold things with their tails. Old World monkeys include baboons, mandrills, macaques, and langur monkeys.

New World monkeys are native to Central America and South America. Most are smaller than Old World monkeys. Their noses are rather flat and their nostrils are far apart. Most New World monkeys are active during the day and sleep at night. Many can hold things with their tails. The group includes marmosets, uakaris, tamarins, squirrel monkeys, spider monkeys, and howlers.

No monkeys are native to the United States or Canada. But we can see monkeys in zoos and circuses. Monkeys are very intelligent. They can be taught tricks and games. They can be taught to help people who must always stay in wheelchairs.

monks and monasteries

A monk is a man who chooses to live apart from the rest of the world for religious reasons. Monks live in places called *monasteries*. Women who choose to live like this are called *nuns*. They live in *convents*.

A monastery may be one building in the middle of a city, or it may have several buildings and large fields in the country. Wherever it is, the monastery is a quiet, peaceful, and often beautiful place. Some are filled with works of art. Others have gardens and fountains. Monks can read, pray, and think about God there.

Monks wear simple clothes, eat simple foods, and do not marry. They try to stay away from anything that could prevent them from thinking about their friendship with God.

Work is an important part of life in a monastery. If the monastery is in the country, the monks may plant crops and raise animals. Some monasteries have their own printing presses and publish books. All monks work together to run the monastery. They cook, clean their rooms, and take care of the gardens and buildings.

The word *monk* comes from the Greek word *monos,* which means "alone." The first Christian monks lived in the deserts of Egypt and Palestine 300 years after Christ's death. Later, monks began to live together in communities in which everyone followed certain rules.

Monasteries were among the few places of learning in Europe during the Middle Ages—especially during the early Middle Ages, sometimes called the Dark Ages. The Middle Ages was a time of change from ancient to more modern ways. Many monasteries of the Middle Ages had great libraries. Monks would spend hours copying books by hand, helping to preserve knowledge from the past. During this time, monks and nuns also started the first hospitals, spending their lives in caring for the sick. (*See* **Middle Ages; Dark Ages;** and **hospital.**)

Other religions besides Christianity have communities of monks. There were Buddhist monks hundreds of years before the birth of Christ. A young Buddhist today may become a monk for a short period before he gets married. Most Buddhist monks live in monasteries. In earlier times, Buddhist monks traveled from town to town, asking others for their food. They were called *holy beggars.* In the Hindu religion, older people who have retired from work sometimes live like monks to fulfill their religious duties.

Monroe, James, *see* **presidents of the U.S.**

A present-day monk studies in the library at Mt. Saviour Monastery in New York state. There are many monasteries and convents in the United States and Canada.

Montana

Capital: Helena
Area: 147,046 square miles (380,849 square kilometers) (4th-largest state)
Population (1980): 786,690 (1985): about 826,000 (44th-largest state)
Became a state: November 8, 1889 (41st state)

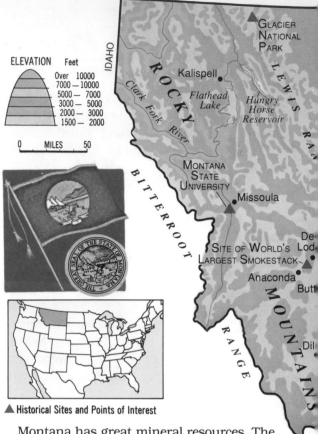

ELEVATION Feet

Over 10000
7000 – 10000
5000 – 7000
3000 – 5000
2000 – 3000
1500 – 2000

0   MILES   50

▲ Historical Sites and Points of Interest

Montana is a state with wide-open spaces and few people. Indians called it the "land of shining mountains." It is also known as "big sky" country.

Montana is in the northwestern United States. It is bordered by Canada on the north, and Wyoming on the south. North Dakota and South Dakota are on the east, and Idaho on the west.

Land The western third of Montana lies in the Rocky Mountains. Forests cover the mountains. Rivers run from them in three directions. Some go north toward Hudson Bay, in Canada. Some go west to the Pacific Ocean. Some go east and south to the Gulf of Mexico. Huge dams have been built across some of the rivers. (*See* **Mississippi River; Missouri River;** and **dam.**)

Glacier National Park is in northwest Montana, on the Canadian border. It has beautiful mountains, about 250 lakes, and more than 50 *glaciers*—slow-moving bodies of ice. (*See* **Glacier National Park.**)

The rest of Montana is in the region called the Great Plains. The land in the central and eastern parts of the state is rolling or hilly and covered with grass. Winters are usually cold—and long. Summers can be very hot in the eastern plains.

The high land in Montana is used for growing timber and for grazing sheep. Beef cattle are raised throughout the state. Wheat and other grains grow on the dry plains.

Montana has great mineral resources. The city of Butte is on top of "the richest hill on earth"—one of the world's largest deposits of copper. Giant machines dig in a pit that is 1 mile (1.6 kilometers) wide and may someday be 2,000 feet (610 meters) deep! The state also contains petroleum, natural gas, and huge deposits of coal.

People There are as few as six people per square mile (2.6 square kilometers) in Montana. Only Alaska and Wyoming have fewer people per square mile. About one out of four Montanans works on a ranch or a farm. Many others are involved in lumbering or mining. Very few Montanans work in factories, because there is little manufacturing in the state.

Even the biggest cities in Montana are not very big. Billings, in the south-central part of the state, is a trade center for the surrounding ranches and oil wells. The mineral refineries and smelters of Great Falls, in western Montana, are powered by electricity from nearby dams. The town of Helena sprang to life when gold was discovered in 1864 in Last Chance Gulch. The gulch—a ravine—is now the main street of this state capital!

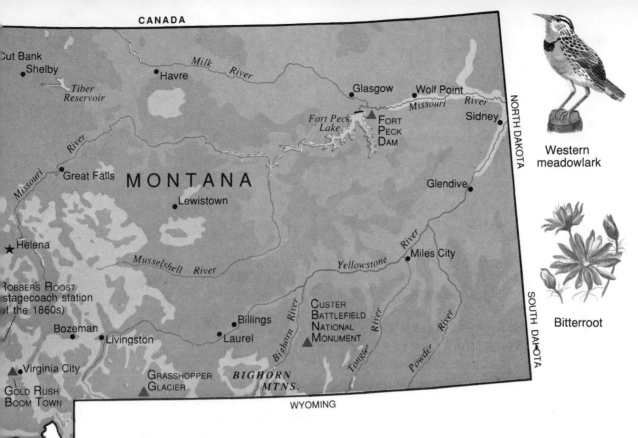

CANADA

Cut Bank
Shelby
Havre
Milk River
Tiber Reservoir
Glasgow
Wolf Point
Missouri River
Fort Peck Lake
FORT PECK DAM
Sidney
NORTH DAKOTA

Missouri River
Great Falls
MONTANA
Lewistown
Glendive

★ Helena
Musselshell River
Yellowstone River
Miles City
SOUTH DAKOTA

ROBBER'S ROOST stagecoach station of the 1860s)
Bozeman
Livingston
Billings
Laurel
Bighorn River
CUSTER BATTLEFIELD NATIONAL MONUMENT
Tongue River
Powder River

Virginia City
GOLD RUSH BOOM TOWN
GRASSHOPPER GLACIER
BIGHORN MTNS.
WYOMING

Western meadowlark

Bitterroot

Cowboys herd cattle in the wide-open spaces of Montana.

History When the first Europeans arrived in Montana in the middle 1700s, they met Blackfeet, Crow, and other Plains Indians in the east, and various tribes of Pacific Coast Indians in the west.

The United States bought most of Montana from France in 1803, as part of the Louisiana Purchase. The rest came as part of the Oregon Territory, which the United States got from Great Britain in 1846. The first planned exploration of the "big sky" country took place in 1805 and 1806, when the Lewis and Clark Expedition arrived. Fur traders followed, and trading posts were built. (*See* **Lewis and Clark Expedition.**)

Buffalo were prized for their hides. This caused white hunters to kill so many that the Indians became angry. They resisted when white settlers began pushing them westward, and there was a lot of fighting between Indians and whites in the 1860s and early 1870s. In 1864, Montana became a territory. Cattle ranching started. As more people came, the Indians tried again to win back the lands they were losing. One of the most famous Indian battles in U.S. history was fought in Montana. In 1876, a cavalry force led by General George A. Custer was sent to quiet the Cheyenne and Sioux. In a fierce battle near the Little Bighorn River, all Custer's troops were killed. The battle is known as "Custer's Last Stand." (*See* **Custer, George Armstrong** and **Indian Wars.**)

Battles continued until late in the 1800s. The Indians eventually lost, and in 1889 the territory became a state. More than 27,000 Indians still live in Montana, most of them on *reservations*—land set aside for them by the U.S. government.

31

Montezuma

Montezuma was a ruler of the Aztec people of Mexico. He headed the Aztec empire when the Spanish invaded in 1519.

Montezuma became emperor of the Aztec in 1502. He was a strong military leader who increased the size of the Aztec empire. Many temples and hospitals were built while Montezuma was the ruler of the Aztec. But he was unpopular because of his many wars and heavy taxes.

In 1519, the Spanish explorer Hernando Cortés landed on the coast of Mexico with about 500 soldiers. Hearing the news, Montezuma thought Cortés was the great Aztec god Quetzalcoatl. The Aztec believed this god had left and promised to return. Montezuma sent presents to the Spanish.

Montezuma was the last great emperor of the Aztec people.

Cortés and his men marched toward Tenochtitlán (tay-NOHCH-tee-TLAHN), the Aztec capital. Along the way, they were joined by Indians who hated the Aztec.

When Cortés arrived, Montezuma welcomed him. A few weeks later, the Spanish took Montezuma prisoner and ruled through him. Not long afterward, the Aztec rose up against the Spanish. Montezuma appeared on a balcony and tried to calm the mob. They showered him with stones. He died shortly after.

See also **Aztec; Cortés, Hernando;** and **Mexico.**

month

A month is a measure of time. In today's calendar, there are 12 months in a year, and each month has between 28 and 31 days.

Why do people measure in months? The word *month* comes from a word for *moon.* Many centuries ago, people noticed that the moon goes through a cycle—a pattern—every 29 or 30 days. On the first night, it is full and round. Each night for about two weeks, it grows smaller, until it seems to disappear. Then, for two more weeks, it grows bigger until it is full once again. (*See* **moon.**)

People began to measure time by how many moon cycles had passed. They would say, "That happened three moons ago."

Our modern calendar was set up by the Roman ruler Julius Caesar in 46 B.C. The months in this calendar do not follow the moon cycle exactly. All the months except February have 30 or 31 days. February has 28 days most years and 29 days in leap years. Together, the days in the twelve months add up to 365 or 366 days—one year.

The Romans gave us the names of our months. January, March, May, and June are named for Roman gods and goddesses. February and April come from the names of Roman religious festivals. July is named for Julius Caesar. August is named for Caesar Augustus, another great ruler of Rome.

NUMBER OF DAYS IN THE MONTH		
	Month	Number of days
	January	31
	February	28 (or 29)
	March	31
	April	30
	May	31
	June	30
	July	31
	August	31
	September	30
	October	31
	November	30
	December	31

The rest of the months have Roman names that stand for numbers. September, October, November, and December mean "seventh," "eighth," "ninth," and "tenth." In the old Roman calendar, the year began with March, and these four months had the right names. Julius Caesar's new calendar started the year in January, and the names of these four months no longer fit. Now they are actually the ninth, tenth, eleventh, and twelfth months of the year.

The table above shows how many days each month has.

See also **calendar.**

Monticello

Monticello was the home of Thomas Jefferson, the third president of the United States. It is built on a hilltop near Charlottesville, Virginia. The name *Monticello* means "little mountain" in Italian. The house rests on about 5,000 acres of wooded land.

Jefferson designed Monticello himself and supervised how it was built. Work began in 1769. Thirteen years later, the two-story house seemed nearly complete. It had 14 skylights in the roof to welcome the sun. In the morning, sun came brightly into Jefferson's bedroom. At day's end, it shone down on the well-furnished dining room.

In 1784, Jefferson went to France as an American minister. He liked the French styles of building. When he returned to Monticello, he added a dome to the top of the house. Monticello was completed in 1809, 40 years after it was begun.

Every year, thousands of people visit Monticello. They see the many gadgets Jefferson invented, such as a calendar clock, a revolving desk, and a machine that made copies of the many letters he wrote.

See also **Jefferson, Thomas.**

Thomas Jefferson, author of the Declaration of Independence, was also an architect. Monticello was his home. He designed it and kept improving it for 40 years.

Montreal

Montreal is the largest city in Canada. It is in Quebec Province, in southeastern Canada. About 3 million people live in and around Montreal. (*See* **Quebec.**)

Montreal is on a large island in the St. Lawrence River. The city was built around an inactive volcano called Mount Royal— Mont Réal in French. Montreal gets its name from this mountain.

Montreal was founded in 1642 as a center for French traders, missionaries, and explorers. During the 1700s, French colonists arrived to farm the surrounding lands. The French settlement grew. But in 1763, France lost the French and Indian War and had to give its Canadian territories to England. (*See* **French and Indian War.**)

For a few months in 1775 and 1776, Montreal was occupied by American revolutionary soldiers. They hoped to make Canada part of the new United States. But the Canadians drove the Americans off.

Montreal grew rapidly in the 1800s, when the St. Lawrence River became an important shipping route. Large oceangoing vessels could sail all the way up the St. Lawrence from the Atlantic Ocean to Montreal. The city developed into a major international port. (*See* **St. Lawrence River.**)

In Habitat, a Montreal apartment complex, apartments are stacked on other apartments.

The British continued to control Montreal until Canada became independent, in 1867. Even today, most Montrealers speak French, and parts of the city have a very French atmosphere. English-speaking people form a large community within Montreal. The city is also home to immigrants from Italy, Germany, China, and many other countries.

The St. Lawrence Seaway opened in 1959. This system of rivers, lakes, and canals links the Great Lakes with the Atlantic Ocean. It has made the city of Montreal one of the world's busiest ports. Crude oil arrives from Venezuela and the Middle East. It is refined in Montreal, then shipped to other places in Canada. Wheat arrives from western Canada and is shipped from Montreal to places around the world. So are the many products manufactured in the city and around it—electrical machinery, canned goods, clothing, and many other things.

The 1967 Universal and International Exposition was held in Montreal. This world's fair, nicknamed "Expo 67," was so popular that a permanent international exhibit was established in Montreal. It is called Man and His World and includes museums, an aquarium, and restaurants. In 1976, the Summer Olympic Games were held in Montreal.

moon

The moon is the biggest and brightest object in Earth's nighttime sky. It has fascinated humans from earliest times. In ancient civilizations, the moon usually held an important place in religion. Also, it was once believed that the moon caused some people to be mentally ill. These people were called *lunatics,* from the Latin word *luna*—"moon." In past centuries, there were popular myths about "the man in the moon." You may also have heard about the moon being made of green cheese. This childhood story got started because cheese is often made in round shapes, and because unripe cheese, called "green cheese," is white, like the moon is.

Astronauts took this photo of the moon when they were on their way to land on it.

Patient study by astronomers over centuries produced a more accurate picture of the moon. By the 1900s, scientists knew a lot about what the moon was really like. On July 20, 1969, the moon became the only body in our solar system, besides Earth, to be visited by people.

Astronomers call the moon a natural *satellite* of Earth. This means that the moon *orbits*—travels around—the earth. It orbits Earth at a distance of about 384,403 kilometers (238,857 miles). Gravity is what keeps the moon in orbit around Earth. Earth is about four times bigger than the moon, so Earth's gravity is strong enough to keep the moon from flying off into a path around the sun.

Although the moon is much smaller than Earth, it, too, has gravity. The moon's gravity is about one-sixth that of Earth. This means that on the moon, you could jump about six times higher than you can on Earth. The moon's gravity affects Earth. It constantly tugs at Earth, making tides rise and fall in our oceans. (*See* **tide** and **gravity**.)

In many ways, the moon is like a planet. With a diameter of 3,480 kilometers (2,160 miles), it is big enough to be a planet. The moon is even larger than Pluto—the planet farthest from the sun—and just a little smaller than Mercury—the planet closest to the sun. But the moon orbits Earth, not the sun, as planets do. So it is a satellite—a moon—and not a planet.

Phases of the Moon   Looking at the moon from Earth, probably its most striking feature is that it appears to change its shape. Over the course of many nights, the moon goes from a narrow crescent to a full, round shining disk, and then back to a narrow crescent again. Then it completely disappears, only to reappear once more as a narrow crescent. These changes are called *phases* of the moon. It takes about 29½ days—almost one month—to complete the phases from one full moon to the next.

PHASES OF THE MOON

New Moon
The moon appears in the night sky as a tiny sliver.

First Quarter
It begins to *wax* — increase in size. In a week, you can see about half.

Full
After two weeks, the moon is a full circle in the sky.

Third Quarter
The moon begins to *wane* — decrease in size. After three weeks you can see about half.

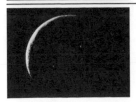

Old Crescent
At month's end, the moon is a tiny sliver, about to disappear.

An astronaut works in his space suit on the moon, setting up experiments.

The moon does not really change its shape—it only looks that way to us here on Earth. It is the same big, round ball of rock and dust throughout the entire cycle of phases. But what does change during the cycle is the amount of the moon's lighted surface we can see here on Earth.

The moon does not produce any light of its own. Instead, it shines by reflecting—bouncing back—the sun's light. No matter what phase we see, the moon is always half-lighted and half-dark. Only the half facing the sun gets lighted. The other half is dark and cannot be seen here on Earth. As you probably know, the same thing happens to Earth. The half facing the sun is lighted while the other half is dark. That is why, when it is daytime for you, it is nighttime for people who live on the other side of the globe.

The moon takes a little more than 27 days to make its trip around Earth. But the earth and moon together are also traveling around the sun. In 27 days, they complete about a thirteenth of this trip. During this time, the sunlight comes from nearly the same direction, but the moon keeps changing its position as it orbits Earth. As the moon moves around behind Earth, sunlight reaches less of the moon's surface. This is what causes the phases we see.

Origin of the Moon Astronomers have long wondered how the moon was formed. Other planets have moons, too, but ours is much larger than most of these other moons. For this reason, people wonder if it was formed in some special way. One idea was that the moon used to be part of Earth but was knocked into space. People thought the hole left behind might have been where the Pacific Ocean is now. Today, we know that the moon is so different from Earth that this cannot be the right explanation. We also know how the Pacific really formed. Another idea is that the moon was once a planet in orbit around the sun. If its path took it close enough to Earth, it might have been captured by Earth's gravity. This idea is hard to disprove, but it seems unlikely.

Today, most scientists believe that the moon formed just the way Earth did, and at about the same time. Scientists think that both Earth and the moon formed from the same cloud of gas, and that they have stayed very near each other ever since. (*See* **earth history.**)

The Surface of the Moon The moon is made of rock and dust. Astronauts who set foot on the moon found a strange and barren world. It is like a desert, completely without water, but also without air. Mountain ranges tower above broad plains. The plains have

Earth rises above the horizon of the moon. It looks blue against the black sky.

many round craters where meteors have struck the moon's surface. Some of the craters are tiny, but some are huge. The largest one is about 1,100 kilometers (700 miles) wide.

The moon's weak gravity cannot hold gases near the moon's surface. As a result, it has no atmosphere. Because there is no atmosphere, there is no weather—no wind, rain, or snow. There are just very hot days and very cold nights. Temperatures on the side of the moon facing the sun can heat up to 127° C (260° F). On the dark side, temperatures can drop to -173° C (-280° F). Astronauts had to stay in their space suits the entire time they were there. The space suits provided air for them to breathe and kept the temperatures livable.

Exploring the Moon For the first space voyage beyond Earth, scientists naturally chose the moon as their destination. The moon is the closest heavenly body to Earth, so the trip would be shorter. That was an important factor. But humanity's long fascination with the moon made the journey that much more important.

On six trips to the moon between 1969 and 1972, astronauts gathered a vast amount of scientific information and saw many unusual sights. They brought back rocks that showed that the moon had not been eroded or changed—except by meteors striking—for billions of years. Some of the rocks were volcanic, showing that at one time the moon was very hot. Looking at the moon's "soil" through microscopes, scientists found tiny glass balls. They have not found any signs of life in the soil.

For the astronauts, perhaps the most memorable sight was their view of Earth, their home, hundreds of thousands of miles away. From the moon's surface, Earth appears to rise in the sky just as the moon seems to do on Earth—only much larger, and a beautiful blue color.

See also **Earth; satellite; solar system; space exploration; meteors and meteorites; and astronaut.**

One of the moon rocks that astronauts brought back for study on Earth.

moose and elk

Moose and elk are the largest members of the deer family. Moose are larger than elk. Moose weigh up to 825 kilograms (1,800 pounds) and stand almost 2 meters (6½ feet) tall at the shoulders. American elk may grow as tall as 1.5 meters (5 feet) and weigh 500 kilograms (1,100 pounds).

These animals live in the forests of North America. Moose also live in northern Europe and Asia. People in different places have different names for the animals. *Moose* is an American Indian name. In Europe, people call this animal an elk. The American elk is a different animal. But early settlers thought it was like the elk in their European homelands. It is less confusing to call the American elk by its Indian name, *wapiti.*

Male moose and wapiti have large, beautiful antlers of solid bone. Every year, in late winter or early spring, the antlers are shed and a new pair grow. The antlers are used to fight wolves, mountain lions, and other enemies. They are also used during the mating season, in autumn, when the males challenge each other. Sometimes, there are fierce fights in which two males attack each other with their antlers.

Females are smaller than males. They do not have antlers. They give birth to one or two young in the spring. They nurse their young and take good care of them until the youngsters are ready to live on their own.

Moose usually live alone. Wapiti live in large groups called *herds.* In summer, the animals live high in the mountains. As winter nears, they move down into valleys, where there is less snow and food will be easier to find. Moose and wapiti eat grasses, twigs, leaves, and other plant matter. If there is a lot of snow on the ground, they may eat the bark off the trees.

A moose has a large head and a thick, strong body. Its coat is brownish black, and it has a dense mane of hair over the shoulders. A flap of skin—called a *bell*—hangs from the throat. The antlers are thick and heavy. They may weigh more than 20 kilograms (44 pounds).

The name *wapiti* means "white rump." This animal has a reddish brown coat with a large pale patch around its tail. The antlers are more branchlike than those of a moose.

See also **deer and antelope.**

Male moose (below right) have large, solid antlers. Wapiti (right) have pointed antlers.

The central temple of the Church of Jesus Christ of Latter-Day Saints (right) is in Salt Lake City, Utah, where members first settled in the 1840s.

Mormons

The Mormons are followers of the Church of Jesus Christ of Latter-Day Saints. Their religion was founded in New York State in 1830 by Joseph Smith. Today, more than 6 million of the world's people are Mormons.

Joseph Smith was the son of a poor Vermont farmer. His family moved to Palmyra, New York, in 1816, in search of better farmland and more work. Mormons believe that during the 1820s, an angel named Moroni appeared to Smith. Moroni told Smith about several solid gold plates that contained the history of ancient peoples in the Americas. Mormons say that Moroni gave the plates to Smith on a hill near Palmyra in 1827. Smith published the writings from these plates in 1830 as the *Book of Mormon.*

In 1831, Smith led a group of his followers west in search of land. They moved first to Ohio, then to Missouri. They finally settled in Nauvoo, Illinois. They built a city that became one of the largest in the state. Many people in Illinois feared the Mormons and did not agree with their beliefs. In 1844, Smith and his brother, Hyrum, were put in jail. An angry mob broke into the jail and killed them. Mormon homes were burned, and their temple was destroyed. The Mormons had to flee.

Brigham Young, their new leader, led the Mormons west from Illinois to Utah's Great Salt Lake Valley in 1847. The Mormons called their new home Deseret. The United States Congress named this area the Territory of Utah and appointed Young its governor in 1850. Mormon settlements in Utah helped the territory grow. Utah became a state in 1896.

Like other Christians, Mormons believe in Jesus Christ. They say that all men and women are the children of God and the brothers and sisters of Jesus. Joseph Smith is considered a prophet. At one time, Mormon men were allowed to have more than one wife. This practice is called *polygamy.* The Mormons outlawed polygamy in 1890, after it became illegal in the United States. Mormons are encouraged by their church to support and follow the laws of the nation in which they live.

Most Mormons today live in Utah and the western states surrounding it. The leader of the church, called the president, lives at the church headquarters in Salt Lake City, Utah. The Mormon Tabernacle, located in Salt Lake City, has a world-famous choir.

Morocco

Capital: Rabat
Area: 172,413 square miles (446,550 square kilometers)
Population (1985): about 23,117,000
Official language: Arabic

Morocco is a country in northwestern Africa, on the Atlantic Ocean and Mediterranean Sea. It has a little more land than the state of California, but not quite as many people.

Children play outside the walls of the old Moroccan city of Marrakech.

The high Atlas Mountains cover much of the central part of the country. South of them is the beginning of the great Sahara Desert. Along the coasts are fertile plains. Farmers there grow wheat and barley as well as vegetables and fruits. They also raise cattle, sheep, and goats. Morocco's large cities are all along its coasts. The biggest is Casablanca, a major port.

Moroccan craftspeople are famous for their work with leather and metal, and for their rugs and pottery. These goods are traded at large city markets called *bazaars.* In the Moroccan countryside, farmers trade goods at another kind of market, called a *souk.*

Almost all Moroccans are descended from the Berbers, the first people to live in the area, or from the Arabs, who conquered it in the 600s and 700s. Morrocans are Muslims—followers of Islam. In the early 1900s, Morocco was controlled partly by France and Spain. It became independent in 1956.

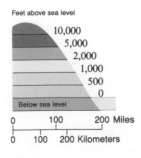

Morse, Samuel F. B.

Samuel Morse developed a successful telegraph and invented the Morse code. He was also an artist.

Morse was born in Charlestown, Massachusetts, in 1791. He studied art in college, along with mathematics, chemistry, and physics. He continued his art studies in London and became a successful artist there.

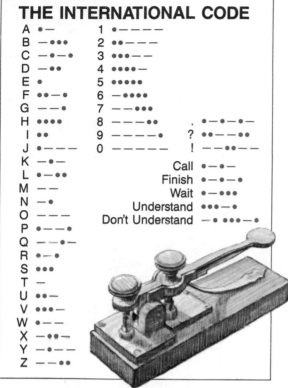

THE INTERNATIONAL CODE

A	•—	1	•————
B	—•••	2	••———
C	—•—•	3	•••——
D	—••	4	••••—
E	•	5	•••••
F	••—•	6	—••••
G	——•	7	——•••
H	••••	8	———••
I	••	9	————•
J	•———	0	—————
K	—•—		
L	•—••	.	•—•—•—
M	——	?	••——••
N	—•	!	——••——
O	———		
P	•——•	Call	•—•—
Q	——•—	Finish	•—•—•
R	•—•	Wait	•—•••
S	•••	Understand	•••—•
T	—	Don't Understand	—••••—•
U	••—		
V	•••—		
W	•——		
X	—••—		
Y	—•——		
Z	——••		

Telegraph operators sent messages in Morse code, in which a letter or number is represented by a group of dots and dashes.

On a voyage back to the United States in 1832, Charles T. Jackson, a doctor, showed Morse a new kind of magnet—the electromagnet. It was an iron bar with wires coiled around it. As soon as the wires were attached to a battery, the rod became magnetic. Without the battery, the rod lost its magnetism. (*See* **magnetism** and **battery**.)

Morse was fascinated with this new invention. As the ship steamed across the Atlantic, he made plans to use electricity and magnetism to send messages.

Morse was not the only one thinking about using electromagnetism to send messages. Joseph Henry, an American scientist, built the first electric telegraph in 1831. In England at about the same time, others used Henry's ideas to build a telegraph. Morse built his first telegraph in 1836.

Morse worked as an artist and taught art at New York University. With Joseph Henry's help, Morse continued to improve his telegraph.

Morse demonstrated his telegraph system in 1837. It was built with electromagnetic

switches that could send and receive electrical signals through wire cables. The signals were long and short bursts of electricity. These are the basis for the *Morse code*—an alphabet of dots, short dashes, and long dashes. A short burst is a dot. A burst twice as long is a short dash. The burst for a long dash is four times that for a dot.

Morse showed his system to the United States Congress. He hoped to get money from the government so he could put his invention to use. In 1843, Congress gave Morse $30,000 to build an experimental telegraph system between Baltimore and Washington, D.C. The system was a success.

In 1861, telegraph wires ran from New York to California. In 1866, the first telegraph cable was laid on the floor of the Atlantic Ocean. Telegraph messages could now be sent from Europe to the United States. The telegraph and the Morse code are still used all over the world.

See also **telegraph**.

mosaic

A mosaic is a picture or pattern formed by setting small pieces of stone, glass, shell, or other materials into glue or cement. Mosaics can also be made of tiles, pearls, seeds, beans, tree bark, or pieces of wood. Pieces with dull, rough textures can be used with

Many small pieces of stone make a picture in this mosaic in Ravenna, Italy.

bright, smooth ones for pleasing effects. People have decorated walls, ceilings, floors, furniture, ships, bathtubs, and pools with mosaics.

People in the Middle East were making mosaics about 5,000 years ago. The ancient Greeks made mosaics, and the Romans learned this art from them. The insides of early Christian churches were covered with mosaics showing religious scenes. Islamic buildings are often covered inside and out with mosaics. Islamic mosaics are arranged in brightly colored patterns.

If you would like to make your own mosaic, plan your design first. Then arrange all the pieces before you begin to glue them down.

Moscow

Moscow is the capital and the largest city of the Soviet Union. With a population of more than 8 million people, it is one of the ten largest cities in the world. It is the center of Soviet government and industry.

Moscow is in the western part of the Soviet Union. It is more than 500 miles (800 kilometers) from the nearest Soviet border. The city was founded in the 1100s. In the 1400s, Russia's ruler, Ivan the Great, made the kingdom of Russia independent. He began building a fortress city, called the Kremlin, at the center of Moscow. In 1547, Ivan's grandson, Ivan the Terrible, became the *czar*—emperor—of Russia.

In the the early 1700s, Czar Peter the Great built a new capital city far west of Moscow, nearer to Europe. He named it St. Petersburg. Moscow was no longer the capital, but it remained an important city.

Great fires have damaged Moscow many times. The worst fire occurred in 1812. A French army commanded by Napoleon had marched all the way to Moscow. Russians may have set their city on fire on purpose to keep it out of Napoleon's hands. Almost all of the city was destroyed. Shortly afterward, the French army retreated.

St. Basil's Church, on Moscow's Red Square, has eight colorful, onion-shaped domes.

In 1917, a revolution ended government by the czars. Soon, the Communist party took control of the country. In 1918, the new government made Moscow the national capital once again. It has remained the capital of the Soviet Union ever since.

Today, the old fortress city, the Kremlin, is where the Soviet government meets. There are still many old buildings and rich treasures in the Kremlin. Just outside the Kremlin walls is Red Square. The large, open square is the scene of many parades and celebrations. It is the center of festivities on May Day—May 1—the most important national holiday in the Soviet Union. The tomb of Lenin, leader of the Russian Revolution, is in Red Square. So is St. Basil's Church, an ancient building with eight onion-shaped domes.

Most people in Moscow live simple lives in small apartments. Many work in factories that turn out hundreds of products, from cars to chemicals. Most people travel by bus or subway. Moscow's subway system is one of the world's best.

Moscow is also famous for its music, dance, and theater. The Bolshoi Ballet is one of the world's great ballet companies. In the summer of 1980, Moscow became the first Russian city to host the Olympic Games.

Moses

Moses was one of the greatest leaders of the Jewish people. He led them from slavery in Egypt. Later, he gave them a set of laws called the Ten Commandments. Christians and Muslims—followers of Islam—follow these laws, too. Moses' story is told in the first five books of the Bible.

Moses was born to a Jewish family in Egypt around 1300 B.C. Hundreds of years earlier, the *Hebrews*—as the Jews were then called—had left their homeland of Canaan to live in Egypt. The Egyptians forced the Hebrews to work as slaves. By the time Moses was born, there were a great number of Hebrews living in Egypt. The Egyptian ruler—*pharaoh*—worried that he would not be able to control them. So he ordered his soldiers to kill all newborn Hebrew boys.

Moses' mother wanted to save her baby. She put Moses in a basket and floated it on the Nile River. The pharaoh's daughter went to the river for a swim, found the baby, and decided to take him home.

Moses' sister had been watching from the riverbank. Now she came out of her hiding place. She said she knew someone who could help care for the baby. As a result,

Moses was raised by his own mother at the pharaoh's palace.

Moses had an Egyptian education, but he never forgot that he was a Hebrew. One day, he saw an Egyptian beating a Hebrew man. Moses killed the Egyptian. Then he fled Egypt and lived as a shepherd. The Bible says that during this time, the voice of God spoke to Moses from a burning bush. God told Moses to return to Egypt and lead the Hebrews to freedom in Canaan.

Moses and his brother Aaron brought God's message to the pharaoh. But the pharaoh would not let the Hebrew people go. The Bible says that God punished the Egyptians, until finally the pharaoh let the Hebrews go. The escape of the Hebrews from Egypt is known as the *Exodus*.

One day, while the Hebrews were camped near Mount Sinai, Moses went up the mountain alone. There, God made a *covenant*—an agreement—with Moses. The Hebrews were to start a new nation called Israel. God would protect them if they lived according to his laws—the Ten Commandments. Years later, Moses and his people reached the land of Canaan and renamed it Israel. Moses died before he set foot on the land.

See also **Bible.**

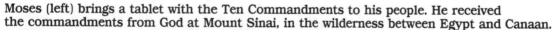

Moses (left) brings a tablet with the Ten Commandments to his people. He received the commandments from God at Mount Sinai, in the wilderness between Egypt and Canaan.

In Grandma Moses' *Sugaring Off*, people collect maple sap to make maple sugar.

Moses, Grandma

Grandma Moses was an American painter. Most famous artists began painting at an early age. But Grandma Moses did not start painting until she was in her seventies. Using bright, clear colors, she painted farm scenes and landscapes. Among her works are *Apple Butter Making* and *Catching the Thanksgiving Turkey*.

Anna Mary Robertson Moses was born in 1860 in Greenwich, New York. She cooked and cleaned for an elderly couple. She married at age 27. She and her husband lived on farms in Virginia and New York and had ten children, five of whom died in infancy.

In 1938, when Grandma Moses was 78, she exhibited her paintings in a drugstore in the small town of Hoosick Falls, New York. An art collector saw the paintings and bought many of them. The next year, she showed her paintings at the Museum of Modern Art in New York City.

Grandma Moses's paintings became very popular. President Harry Truman invited her to the White House in 1949. In 1960, the governor of New York proclaimed her birthday "Grandma Moses Day" in the state. Grandma Moses died in 1961, when she was 101 years old.

mosquitoes and gnats

Mosquitoes and gnats are small, slender flies. On their heads are two long antennae for sensing heat and smells. They have six long, hairy legs, each ending in a pair of claws. They have one pair of wings. Gnats are smaller than mosquitoes.

Female mosquitoes and gnats "bite" by jabbing their mouthparts into the skin of animals or people. Then they suck up their victims' blood. The blood gives them energy to lay eggs. The insect's saliva makes the bite swell and itch. If a gnat or mosquito bites an animal with a disease, it picks up the disease germs. It then spreads the disease to its next victim. Malaria and yellow fever are two human diseases spread by mosquitoes. Heartworm, a disease of dogs, is spread by mosquitoes, too.

Mosquitoes and gnats, like many other insects, have four stages in their life cycles. The eggs are laid in or near water. The eggs hatch into *larvae* that live in the water. During the *pupa*—resting—stage, the larvae change into adults. (*See* **life cycle.**)

People protect themselves from mosquitoes and gnats by using *repellents*—chemicals that keep insects away. People also drain swamps, ditches, and other places where mosquitoes and gnats lay eggs.

mosses and liverworts

Mosses and liverworts are very simple plants that grow close to the ground. They may look like tiny forests only a few inches tall. They usually grow in places that are moist. They may form a green mat over a large rock or along the edge of a stream or pond.

Mosses and liverworts may look like flowering plants, but they are different in important ways. Scientists think they are more like the first plants that appeared on land, especially the liverworts. Like other green plants, mosses and liverworts have chlorophyll, so they can make their own food. (*See* **photosynthesis.**)

If you look at them closely, you will see that mosses and liverworts do not have roots. Instead, they are held to the ground by thin, hairlike structures called *rhizoids.*

They also do not have internal tubes that carry water and food throughout their bodies, as other plants do. This is a major reason why they are so small. They cannot raise water very far from the ground.

Mosses and liverworts do not have flowers or seeds. Instead, they reproduce by spores. First, the plant produces sperm and eggs. When a sperm reaches an egg, a tiny plant develops that is not very much like its parent. It has no chlorophyll, so it gets its food from the parent—the way an embryo gets its food from its mother. Unlike an embryo, however, the tiny plant does not grow up to look like its parent. This plant produces spores. The spores are formed in brown pods at the tops of stalks rising from the tiny plant. The wind blows the spores to new locations. There, they sprout to form new mosses or new liverworts that are like the parent plant.

Mosses and liverworts may look different from each other. Mosses have tiny leaves and stems. Liverworts often look like a single thin, bumpy leaf growing on the ground. Along their edges, some liverworts have structures that look like little cups. Inside the cups are small green circles of plant material. These circles can be carried by the wind to new places, where they grow into new liverworts.

motel, *see* hotels and motels

moth, *see* butterflies and moths

**Left, mosses with spore cases that look like flower buds.
Right, bright green liverwort grows on a tree trunk.**

Mother Goose is pictured riding a goose.

Mother Goose

Mother Goose is the name of a make-believe woman who tells stories and rhymes to boys and girls. Her name often appears on books of *nursery rhymes*—short poems that children have enjoyed for hundreds of years.

Most historians do not believe Mother Goose was ever a real person. The name first appeared in a book published by Charles Perrault in France in 1697. The book contained eight well-known fairy tales. Among them were "Cinderella," "Bluebeard," and "Sleeping Beauty."

Around 1765, a new book called *Mother Goose's Melody* was published in England by John Newbery. This book was a collection of nursery rhymes, including "Little Tom Tucker" and "Old King Cole." Newbery's book was published in Massachusetts in 1786 by Isaiah Thomas. Since then, many collections of Mother Goose rhymes and stories have been printed. Often, they have beautiful pictures. The books have introduced children to such characters as Little Bo Peep, Little Jack Horner, and Jack and Jill.

See also **children's books; fairy tale; poetry;** and **rhyme.**

motion

Motion seems like an easy thing to understand. Motion is movement, and we see movement everywhere. Cars move down the street. Clouds move through the sky. Earth and other planets move through space.

In some ways, motion is more complicated than it seems. In the 1600s, Galileo and Isaac Newton made the first scientific studies of motion. Newton developed three general laws about motion. These laws help us understand many things about it.

The first law says that when an object is *inert*—sitting still—it will remain inert unless a force—such as a push—makes it start moving. If an object is moving, it will keep moving unless a force makes it stop.

Newton's second law is about how much force is needed to start an object moving. The more *mass* an object has, the larger force is needed to start it moving or to stop it. A bowling ball has more mass than a Ping-Pong ball, so it takes more force to get it moving.

The third law of motion: Air rushing out of a balloon in one direction pushes the balloon in the opposite direction.

The third law says that when you apply force to something, there is an equal *reaction* in the opposite direction. When a boat goes forward through water, its propeller is pushing the water in the opposite direction. When a rocket takes off, it produces fire and hot gases. The backward push of the gases forces the rocket forward. (*See* **jet engine.**)

See also **Galileo** and **Newton, Sir Isaac.**

motion pictures, *see* movie; filmmaking

motorcycle

A motorcycle looks something like a bicycle with an engine. In fact, the first motorcycle was a bicycle with an internal-combustion engine on it. It was built by Gottlieb Daimler, a German engineer, in 1885—around the same time that he and Karl Benz were making the first automobiles.

Modern motorcycles may still look a bit like bicycles. But even the smallest ones have frames that are much heavier and stronger than a bicycle's. A motorcycle has to carry more than just the weight of the rider. It must carry the engine, fuel tank, transmission, suspension system, brakes, exhaust system, and other controls.

The *suspension system* lets the motorcycle ride over rough surfaces without bouncing out of control. A motorcycle's wheels are attached to *forks.* Inside the forks are *shock absorbers* to cushion the bumps. The rear wheel also has a rod called a *swing arm* connecting it to the bottom of the frame. As the motorcycle travels over bumps, the swing arm lets the rear wheel move up and down without losing contact with the ground.

The largest motorcycles are called *touring bikes.* They are used for traveling long distances on highways. With their large, wide tires and powerful engines, they can go 100 miles (160 kilometers) per hour and faster. Touring bikes may weigh over 900 pounds (453 kilograms)—a half ton!

Street bikes are built to travel on paved roads, too. But they are smaller and less powerful than touring bikes. Street bikes are used in cities and for short highway trips. Their top speed is about 80 miles (128 kilometers) per hour. Mopeds and scooters are not really motorcycles, but they are meant to be used on paved roads, too.

Trail bikes are powerful, lightweight motorcycles that are used off the road. They are not as fast as street bikes, but they have the power to climb steep hills. They have special tires and suspensions for riding over rugged ground.

Minicycles or *minibikes* are the smallest motorcycles. In most places, they are not allowed on public roads. They are used only for off-the-road recreation.

Motorcycles sometimes have two rear wheels, and sometimes carry a sidecar for an extra passenger.

Motorcyclists must be safe drivers. In most states, they must pass a special driving test—an automobile driver's license is not enough. Most states also require motorcyclists and their passengers to wear helmets for protection.

Below is the first motorcycle ever made. Cycles at right are for highway travel and off-road recreation.

mountain

Mountains are massive bumps and wrinkles on the earth's *crust*—the hard, cold outer shell of our planet. Mountains provide information about events that happened millions of years ago. Scientists look for clues to the earth's long, unwritten history by studying mountains and the rocks that form them. (*See* **earth history** and **geology**.)

Mountains exist singly or in groups. Some groups, such as the Appalachians, form long lines called *ranges*. The longest mountain ranges form *chains* thousands of miles long.

The highest mountain above sea level is Everest. Mauna Kea, in Hawaii, actually begins far under the sea.

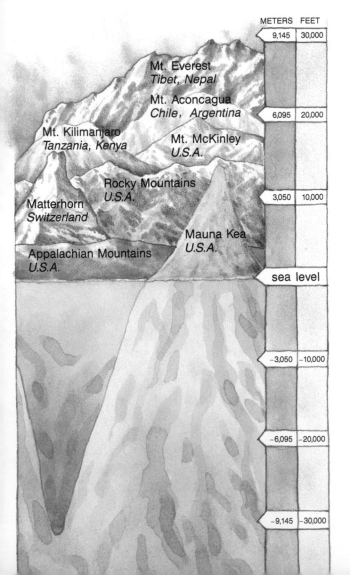

One such chain is the Cordilleras. They stretch from Alaska in North America to the southern tip of South America. In North America, the Cordilleras are made up of the Rockies, the Sierra Nevada, and the Coast and Cascade ranges. In South America, the Cordilleras are made up of the Andes.

Mountains form underwater as well as on dry land. Some of the world's highest mountains are on the floor of the Pacific Ocean. They form a chain over 1,000 miles long. The highest peaks in this chain rise above the surface of the sea and form the Hawaiian Islands. (*See* **island**.)

Formation of Mountains Some mountains, such as those in the Pacific, are volcanoes. They are made of lava and ashes produced by eruptions over many thousands of years. Mauna Kea, on the island of Hawaii, is the highest mountain on Earth. It rises 9,800 meters (32,000 feet) from the floor of the Pacific. The visible part rises 4,300 meters (14,000 feet) above sea level.

Other mountains, such as the Himalayas of central Asia, were created when two plates of the earth's crust pushed into each other. Some of the plates that form the earth's crust carry continents on them. The movement of these plates is called *continental drift*. When two continents drift together, the edge of one is forced under the other. When India began to collide with Asia, more than 50 million years ago, it pushed up the edge of the Asian continent. This created peaks such as Mount Everest, which rises more than 8,800 meters (29,000 feet) above sea level. A mountain range in Europe called the Alps was pushed up when the plate carrying Africa collided with the plate carrying Europe and Asia. (*See* **continental drift**.)

When one plate is forced under another, it is pushed down toward the earth's *mantle*—the layer beneath the crust. In the mantle, temperatures are higher than the melting point of rock. (*See* **Earth**.)

About 40 million years ago, the plate of the Pacific Ocean collided with the North American plate. The edge of the Pacific plate was

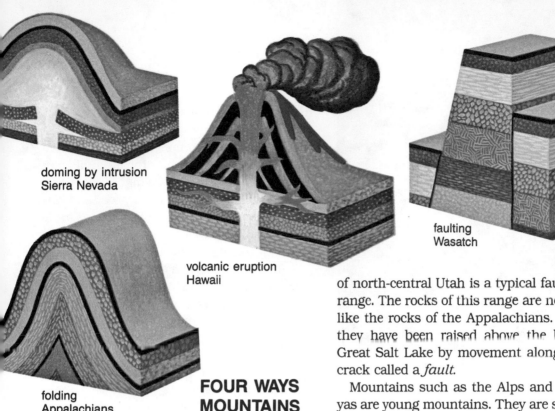

doming by intrusion
Sierra Nevada

volcanic eruption
Hawaii

faulting
Wasatch

folding
Appalachians

FOUR WAYS MOUNTAINS ARE FORMED

pushed under and melted to form new *magma*—melted rock. This magma rose up into the crust, where it cooled off and formed a high range of granite mountains—the Sierra Nevada of California.

About 250 million years ago, the continents of North America and Africa collided. Thick, flat layers of limestone, sandstone, and shale were crumpled into long, straight folds. If you push hard against one edge of a heavy carpet, it will form the kinds of folds that were created in the rocks of eastern North America. Today, the tops of these folds are the long, straight ridges of the Appalachian Mountains in Virginia, West Virginia, and Pennsylvania.

Mountains that form where plates of the crust have collided are raised by *compression*. Compression is a force produced by pushing parts of the crust together. Mountains also form where the crust is being pulled apart. This force is called *tension*. The Great Basin of the southwestern United States is one such area. The mountains that formed in the Great Basin are called *fault-block* mountains. The Wasatch Range

of north-central Utah is a typical fault-block range. The rocks of this range are not folded like the rocks of the Appalachians. Instead, they have been raised above the basin of Great Salt Lake by movement along a deep crack called a *fault*.

Mountains such as the Alps and Himalayas are young mountains. They are still high and rugged. This is because the forces of nature have not had enough time to wear them down. Eventually, *erosion*—the action of wind and water—will reduce even the Alps and Himalayas to low, rounded ridges like the ones we see today in the Appalachian Mountains.

Sharp peaks, such as the Matterhorn in the Swiss Alps, are created by a special kind of erosion called *glaciation*. When two or three *glaciers*—slow-moving, giant sheets of ice—scrape away at different sides of a mountain, only a sharp, horn-shaped peak is left. (*See* **erosion** and **glacier**.)

Eastern U.S. mountains are rounded (left).
Western mountains (right) have sharp peaks.

This surefooted mountain goat lives in Glacier National Park in Montana.

Erosion not only wears mountains down, but creates mountains, too. The Catskills, a group of mountains in New York state, were formed by erosion. The rocks of the Catskills are flat and level, like stacks of pancakes, not folded and crumpled like the rocks of the Alps and Himalayas. For thousands of years, streams in the region cut deeply into a high, flat plateau made of these rock layers. The erosion of the streams has left deep valleys with high, sharp walls. Other mountains created by erosion are the Ozarks of Arkansas and Missouri.

Effects of Mountains Mountains play an important role in life on Earth. They affect weather and climate. High mountains, such as the Cascades and Himalayas, act as a barrier to rain and snow. Most of the moisture in clouds moving east from the Pacific falls on the western slopes of the Cascades. Parts of these slopes are so wet they are called *rain forests.* By the time that Pacific air reaches the other side of the Cascades, there is little moisture left. For this reason, the land east of the mountains is much drier. The same thing happens in Asia, where the Himalayas block moist air from flowing north. As a result, vast deserts, such as the Gobi, have formed behind the Himalayas.

Mountains offer plants and animals a variety of *habitats*—kinds of places to live. The higher you climb up a mountain, the cooler the temperature becomes and the thinner the air. These differences are not very great on low mountains, such as the Catskills. But on higher mountains—such as the Great Smoky Mountains of Tennessee and the Blue Ridge Mountains of North Carolina—the differences are very striking. On the higher peaks, temperatures become so cool and the air so thin and dry that only certain kinds of plants and animals can survive. Above a certain altitude, called the *timberline,* it gets too cold and dry for trees to live. The higher parts of these mountains are almost bare. In the Rockies of Colorado, Montana, and Wyoming, only certain animals can live in the treeless heights above the timberline. Some are small mammals, such as marmots and ground squirrels. Others are hoofed animals, such as mountain goats, that are adapted to life on steep, rocky slopes.

Mountains affect our lives in many other ways. They present obstacles to travel and settlement. They offer opportunities for recreation, such as skiing, hiking, and camping. Many of the world's astronomical observatories are on mountain peaks, because the dry, clear air gives the best view of the heavens. Mountains provide us with minerals and timber, important to modern life.

See the Index for entries on individual mountains.

mountain climbing

Mountain climbing is a popular sport. Most people climb mountains because it is good exercise. It allows them to be outdoors and enjoy beautiful views of nature from great heights. Some climbers climb enormous mountains. For example, many people have climbed Mount Everest—the world's highest mountain—since Sir Edmund Hillary of New Zealand and Tenzing Norgay of Nepal

Rock climbing (left) and snow-and-ice climbing (right) require special training and equipment. Advanced climbers receive training in both types of climbing.

made the first ascent in 1953. But most climbers are satisfied with the challenge of climbing smaller mountains. Mountain climbing is also called *mountaineering.*

There are three basic kinds of mountain climbing. *Rock climbers* climb the steep sides of rocks, cliffs, and mountains. This requires special skills and equipment. Most rock climbers use pitons (PEE-tons)—metal screws with rings on the end. The pitons are screwed into cliffs. Ropes are then attached to the rings to help the person climb.

Snow-and-ice climbers wear boots with *crampons*—spikes—on the bottom. The crampons make it safer for the person to climb slippery surfaces. Snow-and-ice climbers use ice axes to check for loose snow and *crevasses.* Crevasses are deep cracks in the ice or snow. They can be dangerous to the climber because they are often hidden by a thin layer of snow. On high mountains, crevasses can be more than 100 feet deep.

Mixed climbing is a combination of rock climbing and snow-and-ice climbing. Mountaineers who do mixed climbing need lots of experience in both methods.

Mountain climbing is a dangerous sport. Many people have lost their lives on climbs. Winds and storms high in the mountains can be sudden and powerful. Temperatures can fall quickly. To protect themselves from weather and from bad falls, mountaineers use safety equipment and rarely climb alone. Helmets and ropes are two common kinds of safety equipment. Climbers tie ropes around their waists and attach the other end to trees, rocks, or another climber. If a climber slips, the rope breaks the fall.

Climbers must be in good physical shape and must take lessons in the various ways of climbing. These skills are taught at mountaineering clubs. New climbers begin with fairly easy climbs. This way, they can try out all the methods they have learned. After a while, they try climbing higher, more difficult mountains.

Mount Everest, *see* Everest, Mount

Mount McKinley, *see* McKinley, Mount

Mount Rushmore, *see* Rushmore, Mount

Mount Vernon

Mount Vernon was the home of George Washington, the first president of the United States. It is located in Fairfax County, Virginia, near Washington, D.C. Mount Vernon covers about 500 acres of land. It includes a central house and about 15 small buildings.

Work on the main part of the house was started by Augustine Washington in 1732, shortly after the birth of his son George. The house stood at the heart of a 2,500-acre farm. Here, young George spent his boyhood, riding, hunting, and learning to run the large farm.

George's father died in 1743 and left the estate to George's half brother, Lawrence. Lawrence named the house and grounds Mount Vernon in honor of Admiral Edward Vernon, his commander in the British navy. Lawrence died in 1752. George Washington became the owner of Mount Vernon after Lawrence's wife died in 1762.

The house is two and one-half stories high and has 19 rooms. Tall pillars line the front of the house, which faces the Potomac River. The inside is furnished the way it was when George Washington lived there. About 1 million tourists visit Mount Vernon each year.

See also **Washington, George.**

George Washington lived at Mount Vernon before and after he was president.

House mice (top) are usually smaller than kinds that live outdoors (bottom).

mouse

A mouse is a small rodent related to squirrels, rats, and beavers. Rodents have large front teeth for gnawing. These teeth keep growing throughout the animal's life. A mouse's sharp teeth can gnaw through wood.

Mice (the plural for *mouse*) are mammals—the females produce milk for their young. Mice are covered with soft fur, except for their long tails. The tail usually has tiny scales instead of fur. Some species weigh less than ⅓ ounce (10 grams) and are among the smallest mammals.

There are thousands of kinds of mice living all over the world. The most familiar is the *house mouse*. These mice often build nests in buildings and houses. They eat food that people have stored and make nests in clothes and furniture. They may carry germs that cause human diseases. House mice also live in open fields.

The body of a house mouse is about 3 inches (7.6 centimeters) long. The tail is about the same length. Whiskers on the sides of the snout help the mouse feel its way through narrow passages. It has good hearing and poor eyesight.

Female house mice begin to have babies when they are about 45 days old. They may give birth more than five times a year, producing four to seven babies each time. The babies are ready to go off on their own after three weeks.

Many kinds of mice live in fields and meadows. They eat seeds, nuts, and grain crops. They will also eat peas, strawberries, and bulbs.

Deer mice, also called *white-footed mice,* live in forests. They build nests in hollow trees or under logs.

Kangaroo mice live in dry areas in the western United States. They hop about on their hind legs like tiny kangaroos. These mice never drink water. They get all the water they need from the seeds they eat.

If you have pet mice, you must take good care of them. Keep them in a metal cage so they cannot chew their way out. Clean the cage regularly, and cover the bottom with wood shavings or cat litter. Add a handful of hay so the mice can make a bed. The cage should also have ladders and an exercise wheel. Feed your mice grains, seeds, and small amounts of fresh vegetables once or twice a day. Attach a water bottle to the cage, and change the water every day.

Be very gentle when you hold a pet mouse. Never pick it up by its tail. (*See* **pets.**)

movie

Movies—also called *motion pictures*—are a favorite form of entertainment all over the world. Different kinds of movies have been popular at different times. During wartime, movies about war and spies become favorites. But so do comedies and musicals, movies that help people forget their troubles for a while. In today's era of space exploration, movies about outer space—such as the *Star Wars* and *Star Trek* movies—attract large audiences. Moviemakers also realize that teenagers have become a large and important audience for movies. Teen films featuring popular music and young stars are a major part of today's movie industry.

Westerns have been favorites in good times and bad. People of all ages, all over the world, seem never to tire of these tales of the cowboys and Indians of America's "Wild West." Good mysteries and thrillers, too, can be counted on to attract large audiences. Although most people do not like feeling afraid in real life, they find scary movies exciting.

Moviemakers use special photo effects to create imaginary machines or monsters. These land-walkers from *The Empire Strikes Back* are a good example.

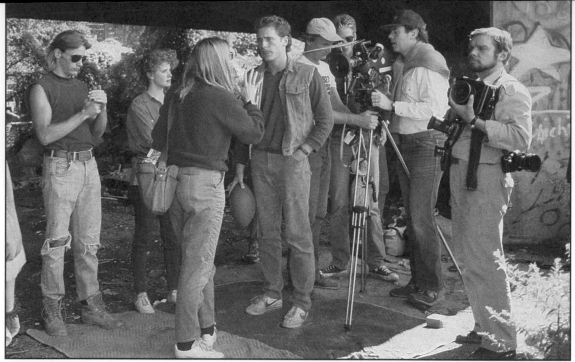

A movie crew gets ready to shoot a scene. Foot markings show actors where to stand. Cameras, lights, and microphones are prepared and tested.

People respond to movies so well that movies are also very effective educational tools. Government, business firms, schools, and hospitals use movies to teach important information in an enjoyable way.

Planning a Movie The people who first get a movie started are usually the *producer* and the *director*. The producer helps raise money, and the director is in charge of actually making the movie. The director gathers all the experts, discusses the movie with them, plans rehearsals, and makes a schedule for filming.

Before the first scene can be filmed, the producer and director must do a lot of planning. They must hire actors and arrange for scenery and costumes to be ready. They must decide where and how the movie will be filmed. Parts of it may be filmed *on location*—a place such as a city street or a seaside town. If the movie will be filmed on location, the director and his or her helpers have to make plans to move people and equipment to the location.

The *set designer* makes the scenery for the movie. For one scene, a set designer may create a forest. For another, he or she may create a spaceship control room or a room in a castle. The set designer's helpers find or

make the right furniture, pictures, and other *props* for each scene.

The set designer works closely with the *lighting director*. Depending on how the lights are set, a scene can look bright and cheery or dark and scary. The same set may be lighted differently for day scenes and night scenes.

Other people plan costumes for the movie. Will the actors need torn blue jeans and T-shirts? Will they need armor or space suits? The *costume director* finds all the right costumes or has them made. He or she also makes sure that the costumes are kept clean, and has them repaired if they are damaged.

The *makeup director* plans makeup for the actors. Actors nearly always need some makeup to appear natural under bright lights. In some movies, actors may need makeup to look much older or younger, or perhaps to turn into monsters.

Filming the Movie When all the planning has been done, it is time to begin filming. This takes the work of many other people with special filmmaking skills. To learn more about them, *see* **filmmaking**.

On a filming day, all the people involved in the scheduled scenes gather in the place

During the scene, a close-up on characters' faces shows what they are feeling. Later, the camera may pull back to show action.

where the scenes will be filmed. The actors are in their costumes and makeup, ready to play their roles. (*See* **actors and acting**.)

During filming, the director tells the actors where to stand or sit, how to speak their lines, and what movements to make. The director also pays attention to the lighting, the sound, and all the other ingredients of the scene. If anything goes wrong, the director has the scene filmed again and again until everything is right.

Putting the Movie Together   The scenes of a movie story are usually not filmed in the order in which the audience sees them. For example, all of the outdoor scenes may be filmed one day. The indoor scenes may be filmed weeks later on a soundstage. When all of the movie has been filmed, all of the scenes must be put together in the proper order. The director and the *film editor* must decide which scenes to use and which ones to cut.

They also choose different camera angles. A scene where two people are talking would not be very interesting if it were filmed by one camera that never moved. With three different camera angles, the film editor may show both people, then a close-up of one face, and next a close-up of the other face.

The angles help you keep track of who is speaking and what is important.

As the film is being put together, the sound director adds new sounds. This is also the time to put in background music. The music can make a scary scene even scarier. A person called a *sound mixer* puts all the sounds together on one sound track.

The film editor takes scenes filmed at different times and by different cameras and fits them together to tell a story.

Movie History The first movies were projected on a screen for the public to see in 1895, in Paris, France. Thomas Edison, the famous U.S. inventor, developed a better projector and used it to present the first movies to the public in the United States the following year. (*See* **Edison, Thomas Alva.**)

At first, people were excited just to see figures moving on the screen. But they did not become really interested until movies began telling stories, in the early 1900s. After that, making movies became a major industry. A small town in southern California called Hollywood quickly became the movie capital of the world.

Until the 1920s, movies were silent. The pictures told the story, sometimes with the help of written words. A phonograph or a piano or organ player in the theater played music to fit the mood of each scene.

There were silent melodramas, silent comedies, and silent westerns. Because the movies had no sound, they all had to have plenty of action to keep audiences interested. Many great silent comedies were made. They featured such favorites as the Keystone Cops, Buster Keaton, and one of the greatest actors of all time—Charlie Chaplin. Many of the best silent films are still shown today. The melodramas, which audiences used to take very seriously, often make us laugh today. The gestures and facial expressions used by the actors to show strong feelings look unnatural and rather silly to modern audiences. (*See* **melodrama.**)

When movies began to include sound, many favorite silent movie stars were suddenly no longer popular. In the "talkies," their voices were not very attractive. New stars took their places.

New moviemaking techniques were introduced, including color film. Today, movies are considered an art, like writing or painting. But unlike a piece of writing or a painting, making a movie may require the work of hundreds of people.

In the 1920s, movies had no sound of their own. A movie-house pianist played music to accompany the movie and increase the audience's enjoyment.

When all the pieces are together, it is time to show the movie to an audience. Was it funny? Was it scary? Was it exciting? The audience gets to decide.

Mozambique, *see* Africa

Mozart, Wolfgang Amadeus

Wolfgang Amadeus Mozart (MOAT-zart) was one of the most amazing musicians who ever lived. He was born in Austria in 1756. By the time he was only five years old, he was playing concerts all by himself on the harpsichord—an instrument that is something like the piano.

Mozart began performing and composing music when he was only five years old!

Wolfgang's father, Leopold Mozart, was also a musician and composer. He took his talented young son to many cities in Europe and arranged for him to play for kings and nobles. For part of the year, father and son traveled. The rest of the year, they were at home in Austria with Wolfgang's mother and sister.

Mozart soon began to write music as well as play it. By the time he was eight, orchestras were playing his compositions. He spent the rest of his life playing and composing music. He wrote more than 40 symphonies for orchestras to play, and many concertos for piano and orchestra. He also wrote operas, including *The Marriage of Figaro,* still one of the most popular in the world.

Mozart had many disappointments and never earned a very good living. He died in 1791, when he was only 35 years old.

Muhammad

Muhammad was the founder of the religion called Islam. Followers of Islam are called Muslims or Moslems. The Muslim word for God is *Allah.* Muhammad is known to all Muslims as the "prophet of Allah."

Muhammad was born around the year 570 in the city of Mecca, in the present-day country of Saudi Arabia. His father died before Muhammad was born, and his mother died when he was very young. He grew up in the home of his grandfather. Mecca was a busy trading center at this time. Merchants came to the city leading their *caravans.* These were long "trains" of pack animals, such as camels and mules. The animals carried goods for trade on their backs.

As a boy, Muhammad listened to the merchants talking in the languages of their different countries. From them, he learned about the customs of other lands. Muhammad later worked as a camel driver on a caravan. He became a successful businessman, then married and started a family.

Muslims believe that around this time, the angel Gabriel appeared to Muhammad. The angel told Muhammad to spread God's word among the people.

Muhammad began preaching his message to the people of Mecca. He told them there was only one God, named Allah. He said that people should treat each other with respect, and that they must care for the poor.

Many people in Mecca did not agree with Muhammad. They were afraid that if they changed their way of living, merchants would no longer bring their caravans to Mecca. The city would become poor. As a result, the rulers of Mecca attacked Muhammad and his followers.

These pilgrims come to Mecca to see where Muhammad first taught.

Muhammad and his family were forced to leave Mecca. They traveled to Medina, a nearby city. Muslims call this journey the *Hegira*. The Muslim calendar begins with this event.

The people of Medina welcomed Muhammad and made him their leader. Muhammad made laws that helped the poor and that required people to worship only one God. Then the cities of Mecca and Medina went to war. Muhammad proved himself a skillful warrior. The city of Mecca surrendered to him in the year 630. Muhammad died in Medina in 632.

Muhammad's teachings were written down by his followers and collected to make a book called the *Koran*. It remains the most holy book of Islam today.

See also **Islam.**

Muhammad Ali, *see* Ali, Muhammad

multiplication, *see* arithmetic

mummy

A mummy is a dead body that has been specially treated to prevent it from decaying. The word usually refers to human bodies preserved and wrapped in fine strips of linen by the ancient Egyptians, thousands of years ago. (*See* **Egypt, ancient.**)

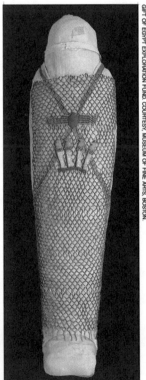

A mummy (right) is a preserved body wrapped in cloth. Some were placed in beautiful painted cases like the one below.

The Egyptians thought that people who died would live new lives in a place called the *underworld*. In this next life, they would still need their earthly bodies. So the Egyptians worked out a detailed method of preserving the body with chemicals.

It took the Egyptians about 70 days to make a mummy. First, the brain was removed through a nostril. Then, through a cut in the body, the lungs, stomach, and intestines were removed. The heart and kidneys were left inside. The removed body parts were preserved in a separate jar or box. The body might be filled with sawdust, linen rags, or resin. Next, the body was placed in a solution of *natron*—sodium carbonate—for several weeks to dry it out. After this, the body was washed, rubbed with oil, and then wrapped in layers of clean linen cloth. Finally, it was placed in a decorated coffin for burial. Everyday objects were buried with the dead for use in the next life. Mummies were also often made of animals that the Egyptians considered holy—such as cats.

mumps

Mumps is a disease that attacks the salivary glands. It makes the glands in the cheeks swell painfully. It also causes pain and swelling below and in front of the ears. Children from five to ten years old are most likely to get the disease, if they have not been vaccinated. (*See* **vaccine.**)

Mumps is caused by a virus that can spread from one person to another. Some people who are infected with the virus do not get sick. But they can still infect others.

The first signs of mumps appear about 18 days after the virus enters the body. The person develops a fever, headache, and muscle aches. Then the glands become sore and swollen, making it difficult to chew or swallow. The swelling lasts about a week.

The disease sometimes infects other parts of the body. Then it can be very serious. If the nerves are attacked, very high fever, severe headache, and vomiting occurs.

Mumps is usually not dangerous in children, but can be serious in adults. Adults who have never had mumps should be vaccinated to protect themselves. One good thing about mumps is that if you do catch it, you usually will not ever get it again.

muscle

Think of all the different ways you can move your body. You can walk, run, jump, skip, and throw. You can wiggle your nose, fingers, and toes, blink your eyelids, and open and close your mouth. Your muscles make all these movements possible. Muscles also move food through your stomach and intestines and keep your heart beating. Messages received from nerves tell muscles exactly what to do. (*See* **nerve.**)

Muscle is tough, elastic tissue made of long, flat cells. Individual muscle cells have the ability to *contract*—shorten. The more muscle cells that contract, the harder the muscle can pull. In your arm, more muscle cells contract when you lift a heavy object than when you lift a light object.

Your muscle cells need energy to contract. They burn a sugar called *glucose* for energy. Muscle cells need oxygen to burn sugar. Both glucose and oxygen are supplied by the bloodstream.

Muscles have different jobs. Skeletal muscles move the body. Smooth muscles move internal organs. Cardiac muscles help pump blood in the heart.

skeletal   smooth   cardiac

There are three kinds of muscles. *Smooth muscles* are in some of the body's organs. The stomach, intestines, blood vessels, and bladder all contain smooth muscles. Smooth muscles slowly contract and relax without your having to tell them to. The contracting and relaxing of the smooth muscles in the stomach and intestines move food along as it is digested. Muscles in the blood vessels keep the blood moving through your body.

Cardiac muscles are only in the heart. They are constantly contracting and relaxing. You feel them moving as your heart beats.

Skeletal muscles are the muscles attached to the bones of your skeleton. You tell your skeletal muscles when and how to move. Skeletal muscles work in pairs. One muscle bends a joint, and another muscle straightens it out. For example, feel the muscle in your upper arm as you bend your arm back and forth. When the muscle in the front of your upper arm—the *biceps*—contracts, your elbow bends. When the muscle in the back of your upper arm—the *triceps*—contracts, your elbow straightens.

To keep your muscles healthy, it is important to do three kinds of exercise. One kind involves stretching. When you do stretching exercises, the muscles become more flexible.

When the muscles under the arm contract, the arm straightens out. When the muscles on top contract, the arm bends.

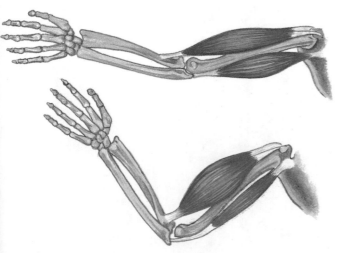

Then you can bend and move more freely and are less likely to injure your muscles. When you do exercises such as weight lifting, your muscle cells get bigger. When you do exercises such as jogging or swimming, the muscles in your heart and blood vessels become stronger. If muscles are not used, they grow weak. Exercise helps keep the muscles strong and healthy.

museum

Do you want to know about animals and plants—where they live and what they look like? Are you interested in dinosaurs or life in colonial America? Would you like to know how American Indians once lived—what they wore, how they found food, what kinds of things they made? You can learn about all of these things in museums.

A museum is a place where a collection of objects is kept for people to see and study. Some museums—such as the Smithsonian Institution in Washington, D.C., the Museum of Science and Industry in Chicago, and the Royal Ontario Museum in Toronto—are very large and have many kinds of collections. Other museums—such as the Museum of Westward Expansion in St. Louis and the Southwest Museum in Los Angeles—concentrate on one subject or on a group of closely related subjects. There are science museums, history museums, special-purpose museums, and art museums. (*See* **art museum**.)

All museums have objects on display. Many museums also have some objects that are not on display. Some of these are studied by experts and advanced students. Others are displayed only for special *exhibitions*— shows. Items may be stored because the museum has more objects than it can show at one time. Other objects may be too delicate to be on display all the time. Museums protect their treasures by controlling light, temperature, and dampness.

Today's museums offer a variety of activities. Museum guides take groups of people

A worker in a science museum puts together casts of dinosaur bones.

of all the objects in the museum. *Curators* learn about the history of each object and plan exhibits. *Conservators* use special methods to clean and repair objects. *Designers* build display cases and install wiring to light exhibits attractively.

Science Museums Some of the earliest museums were science museums. People collected plants, animals, or rocks and placed them on shelves or in cabinets. Cards or labels gave information about the objects. Some science museums had drawings of plants, animals, rocks, or machines.

Science museums, such as the American Museum of Natural History in New York, now group objects with something in common. Labels on a bird exhibit, for example, may tell which birds are related to one another, where they live, how their eggs differ, and what they eat.

through the collection and explain why the objects are interesting or important. Some museums show movies or give talks about the objects in their collections. Many museums offer classes, too.

Skilled people are needed to help run museums. The museum *registrar* keeps records

Some science museums have exhibits that people can touch and move, so that they can learn by doing. These displays help explain hard-to-understand ideas about things like light and color, motion, and machines.

Art Museums Art museums have drawings, paintings, sculptures, and other forms

At the Ontario Science Centre, visitors can look at things under a microscope.
At the Smithsonian Air and Space Museum, visitors can examine many kinds of aircraft.

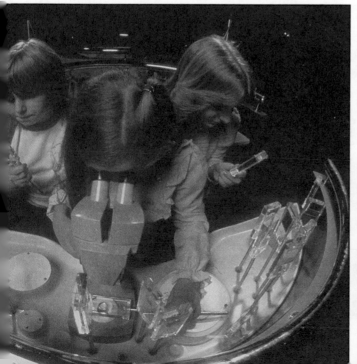

of art. Some museums, such as the Metropolitan Museum of Art in New York and the Museum of Fine Arts in Boston, display art from different countries and times. Others show works from just one time or place, or by just one artist. The Museum of Modern Art in New York City has art from the 1840s to the present. The Rodin Museum in Philadelphia has sculpture by the French artist Auguste Rodin.

History Museums People visit history museums to see how people lived in earlier times. A history museum may be one building—or a whole village! George Washington's home in Mount Vernon, Virginia, is now a museum. The house and grounds are kept the way they were when Washington's family lived there 200 years ago. Colonial Williamsburg, also in Virginia, is a museum town. It shows how colonists lived in the 1700s.

Some museums are partly history museums. The Heard Museum of Anthropology and Primitive Arts in Phoenix, Arizona, has American Indian exhibits. Some show Indian history, and others display Indian works from our time.

The Circus World Museum in Wisconsin has many exhibits and shows about the circus.

Special-Purpose Museums Many newer museums are concerned with one subject. For example, The Museum of Broadcasting in New York City has a collection of television shows. People go there to watch old shows. There are many museums about individual sports and their history. The National Baseball Hall of Fame and Museum in Cooperstown, New York, is one example. A museum may be about any subject at all—crafts, railroads, dogs, games, or toys. There are even circus museums, such as the Ringling Museum of the Circus in Sarasota, Florida, and the Circus World Museum in Baraboo, Wisconsin.

History of Museums The word *museum* comes from the Greek word *museion,* which means "a place for the works of the Muses." The Greeks believed that the Muses were goddesses who inspired people to create poetry, music, dance, and other arts. A Greek *museion* was a temple to the Muses. It was mainly for students and scholars.

For many centuries, kings, church officials, and wealthy people collected works of art and other objects. But not until the 1600s did some people open their collections to the public. Many museums grew when people gave them their collections. Today, museums also buy objects to add to their collections, or borrow from other museums for special shows.

Children's museums are a modern invention. Children's museums have "hands-on" exhibits—collections of things that you are allowed to handle, play with, or even climb upon!

mushroom

A mushroom is a kind of fungus. The mushroom is the part we see above the ground. It contains the reproductive parts of the fungus. Fungi grow in warm, moist places. They take food from dead materials in or on the soil. (*See* **fungus.**)

A mushroom begins as a tiny spore that looks just like a speck of dust. When the

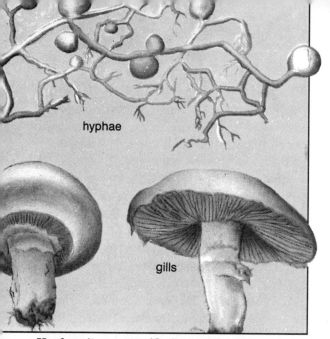

hyphae

gills

Hyphae (top, magnified) grow in soil. Mushrooms (bottom) grow from the hyphae.

spore sprouts, many tiny threads called *hyphae* grow from it. The hyphae usually grow underground.

When spores of one kind of mushroom sprout, their hyphae grow outward and form a circle. Mushrooms grow from the outer edge of the circle. The result is a ring of mushrooms called a "fairy ring."

On the underside of a mushroom's cap are many tiny slits, called *gills*. Spores form on the gills. When the spores are ripe, they are released from the mushroom and carried away by the wind. If the spores land in a warm, moist spot, they will sprout and more mushrooms will grow.

A mushroom can grow very quickly, since its main body has lived for a long time underground. One day, you see nothing. The next day, after a rain, you may see fully grown mushrooms in a grassy spot or on a rotted log. The mushrooms will live as long as they have food or until they have produced spores.

Some mushrooms are easily recognized because they are shaped like an umbrella. But not all mushrooms have this shape. Some look like brown balls between the size of a Ping-Pong ball and a tennis ball. If you step on them, you may see a cloud of "dust" shoot from them. The "dust" is the spores. These mushrooms are called *puffballs*.

Some mushrooms are brightly colored and look so much like ocean corals that they are called *coral mushrooms*. Other mushrooms are shaped like empty cups and have such names as *brown cup, elf cup,* and *blueberry cup. Scarlet cup* is a bright red, cup-shaped mushroom.

Bird's nest mushrooms are also shaped like cups, but they have round bumps, like eggs, in the cups. These mushrooms often grow on dead leaves. They are less than an inch (2.5 centimeters) across. The "eggs" in these mushrooms produce spores.

Many people like to eat mushrooms. Some people collect them in the woods. But some mushrooms are poisonous. One very pretty mushroom has a red or orange cap with white spots. This is the poisonous *fly amanita*. The *destroying angel* is the most poisonous mushroom of all. It is white with raised white spots.

CAUTION: Never pick and eat wild mushrooms. Only an expert can tell which mushrooms are safe to eat.

Below, a fairy ring of mushrooms. Hyphae have grown from the center outward in all directions. Right, a fly amanita— a mushroom that is beautiful to look at but very poisonous.

Singing may have been the first music. It is still a favorite form of music.

music

We hear so much music in a week that we may not even notice some of it. Some days, you may hear a school band or orchestra, or hear music in a church. You may play music from records and tapes, or hear music on the radio. You hear background music during television shows and movies. Many radio and television commercials use music.

People make their own music, too. Whenever you hum or whistle a tune, you are making music. Classes and choirs sing together. Many boys and girls study to become good musicians. They may take singing lessons or learn to play a musical instrument.

In some ways, music is a language. People use it to express moods and feelings. Some music is happy, and some is sad. Some is serious, and some can make people laugh. Many popular songs are love songs.

Some music is used for special occasions. On a birthday, everyone sings "Happy Birthday to You." Special songs are played at weddings. We hear marches and patriotic songs on the Fourth of July and other national holidays. We sing Christmas carols around Christmas.

Elements of Music There are three important elements to music—rhythm, melody, and harmony. All music must have at least one of these elements. Most of the music we hear has all three elements.

Rhythm is a pattern of beats. We can tap out a rhythm with our foot or clap our hands. Drums, cymbals, triangles, and tambourines are among the many instruments used mostly to give rhythm to a musical piece played by a group. (*See* **rhythm.**)

Melody is a pattern of high and low tones played one after the other. You can whistle or hum a melody. Most musical instruments can play melody. (*See* **melody.**)

Harmony is made up of two or more tones played at the same time. The instruments of an orchestra or band make harmonies when different instruments play different notes at the same time. A piano or an organ can produce harmony by itself if the player strikes more than one note at the same time. (*See* **harmony.**)

Folk Music Folk music is one of the oldest kinds of music. We often do not know who first made up folk tunes. They were played and sung for years before someone wrote them down. Parents taught the songs to their children. When the children grew up, they taught the songs to *their* children. Travelers spread the songs from village to village. We still learn folk songs in family gatherings, camps, and schools.

Folk songs often tell stories—about a place, about people in love, or about heroic adventures. Some folk music was for religious holidays. For example, some Christmas carols tell the story of the birth of Jesus Christ. Singing Christmas carols is part of the celebration of Christmas. (*See* **folk song.**)

Not all folk music is for singing. For example, in Scotland and Ireland, very old bagpipe music is played during celebrations and dancing. In the United States, there are very old songs for guitar, mountain dulcimer, and fiddle—another name for the violin.

Written Music We know that people have had music for thousands of years. We have ancient pictures of people singing, playing musical instruments, and dancing. But they did not have a way to write their music down or record it. For this reason, we do not know what their music sounded like.

About 900 years ago, church musicians in Europe invented a way to write down the music they played. Their new invention was *musical notation*—written symbols showing how to play the music. Over the centuries, people made changes in the notation system. Gradually, it became the system we use to-day. We put round *notes* on five parallel horizontal lines called a *staff*. Where the notes are placed tells their pitch.

Composers—men and women who wrote music—signed their names on their work, so people knew who they were. Composers who wrote beautiful or interesting music were re-membered. Their music could be played again and again in the same way, even hundreds of years later.

Classical Music Musical notation made it easier for composers to write very compli-cated music. They could write different parts for different voices or musical instruments. Then all the performers could read their own parts and play together. We often call

complicated music from past centuries *clas-sical music*.

Today, a piano student is likely to learn pieces by such classical composers as Bach, Mozart, and Beethoven. People go to concert halls in cities and towns to hear music by these and other classical composers. This music may include *symphonies, concertos, sonatas*, and many other forms of music. (*See* **Bach, Johann Sebastian; Beethoven, Ludwig van; Mozart, Wolfgang Amadeus; symphony;** and **concerto.**)

Another kind of classical music is *opera*. An opera is a play in which the characters sing part or all of their words. The singers usually wear costumes and act out the story. (*See* **opera.**)

Improvised Music Not all music is writ-ten down and then learned. From earliest times, performers have made up music while they were playing. This music is called *improvised music*. Improvised music is never sung or played the same way twice.

Folk-music and rock-music performers of-ten improvise when they play. Many great classical musicians were great improvisers. Bach, Mozart, and Beethoven often per-formed on keyboard instruments similar to

A single musician can play many parts at once on a large pipe organ (left).
The musician at right enjoys making music in a school band.

Banjo bands were especially popular in the United States in the late 1800s.
Today, banjo bands play old favorites outdoors in the summertime.

the piano. At performances, they often composed a piece as they went along. Since there were no recordings in those days, we can never know exactly how these great musicians played when they improvised.

Since the early 1900s, a new kind of improvised music called *jazz* has grown up. It began in the United States and comes from earlier music performed by black Americans. Today, people play jazz in many parts of the world.

All the performers in a jazz group know the same songs. When they are playing together, different members of the group get to play solos. Each soloist improvises, using imagination and skill to play the song in a new way. (*See* **jazz.**)

Recorded Music In the early 1900s, a new invention—the phonograph—changed the way we think about music. The phonograph made it possible to record musical performances and listen to them again and again. People who wanted to learn to improvise could learn by listening to records of other improvisers. Many jazz musicians learned this way. Recordings made written music less important. Hearing how a piece is played is better than just reading the notes printed on paper. (*See* **phonograph.**)

Soon, many people had phonographs and could buy records. Radio began sending out music so that even people who lived in very small towns could hear the best musicians in the world. A great bandleader and composer, like Duke Ellington, could become famous. His band was a favorite of millions who never heard the band in person. But they heard it on the radio and on records. (*See* **Ellington, Duke.**)

Recordings and broadcasting brought all kinds of music to listeners. People who liked classical music could buy records of performances by soloists and orchestras they might never hear live. On the radio, a different opera was broadcast every Saturday. Soon there were many new opera fans.

Popular Music Recordings, radio, and television made several kinds of music popular in the United States. There was a "Hit Parade"—a list of the most popular songs in the nation. People throughout the country could be humming the same popular song at the same time.

Much of the earlier popular music was for dancing. Then in the 1950s, a new kind of music called *rock 'n' roll* began. For years, it was the most popular music, especially for young listeners. (*See* **rock music.**)

Special Music Today, people use music in a variety of ways. In advertisements on radio and television, special songs called *jingles* help us remember the names of products. In a movie, background music gives the audience clues to the story. It can tell you when to be nervous, when to be sad, and even when to laugh. Background music is played in many stores and offices, too. Dentists have learned that quiet music can calm people's fears. Storekeepers play music to put people in a better mood and encourage them to buy more.

Careers in Music Thousands of people work at musical careers. Most of them are music teachers. They teach individual students and classes how to play instruments and to sing. Others lead bands, orchestras, or choirs. They may also write music or build musical instruments.

Skilled musicians may perform in groups, such as rock bands, dance bands, orchestras, or choruses. A few of the very best musicians become soloists. They may sing the lead roles in operas, give solo concerts, or become stars of popular music.

Millions of people make a hobby of performing or listening to music.

musical instrument

A musical instrument is anything that can make musical sounds. There are hundreds of musical instruments. They come in a variety of shapes, sizes, and materials. Each instrument and group of instruments has its own special sound. We call this sound its *tone color.* (*See* **sound.**)

Some instruments are small enough to carry around in a pocket. One example is the recorder—a simple, whistlelike instrument about 8 inches (20.5 centimeters) long.

Some instruments are so large and complicated that they cannot be carried around at all. In fact, they cannot be moved from the place where they were built. For example, a large pipe organ is usually built into a concert hall or a church. People who want to play a particular pipe organ travel to it.

Musical instruments are divided into five families. Understanding each of the families is the simplest way to learn about the different instruments.

Instruments around the world (clockwise from top left): steel drums (West Indies), bagpipe (Scotland), pressure drum (Africa), dulcimer (U.S.), and sitar (India).

Woodwind Instruments There are many instruments in the woodwind family. They are called woodwinds because all of them used to be made of wood and they are played by blowing. The player changes the pitch of the notes—how high or low they are—by covering and uncovering holes along the instrument's body.

The *recorder* is a simple woodwind. A player makes a sound on a recorder by blowing into it like a whistle. In fact, a recorder is a kind of whistle.

In other simple woodwind instruments, the player blows across a hole, instead of blowing directly into a mouthpiece. The sound is produced by air vibrating through the instrument. Two instruments that work this way are the *flute* and the *piccolo*. Both these instruments are played by holding them sideways to the right of the face. The flute is the larger instrument and has a mellow, warm tone. The piccolo is much smaller and plays the highest notes in the orchestra. Today, most flutes and piccolos are made of metal instead of wood.

Woodwind instruments: tenor saxophone (left), bassoon (top center), clarinet (bottom center), and flute (right).

Another large group of woodwinds uses *reeds,* made from a plant. One or two reeds are attached to the mouthpiece. When the player blows through the mouthpiece, the reeds vibrate. The *oboe* and *bassoon* are *double-reed* instruments. The oboe has a strong, piercing voice. The bassoon, a much larger instrument, has one of the lowest voices in the woodwind family.

The *clarinet* has a single reed. The clarinet plays about the same pitches as the oboe, but has a more mellow tone color. It is used in most orchestras and is an important instrument in marching and concert bands. Another single-reed instrument is the *saxophone.* Three saxophones—alto, tenor, and baritone—are often used in jazz bands. The saxophone was invented around 1840 by Adolphe Sax.

One unusual woodwind instrument is the *bagpipe.* The piper blows lots of air into a bag held under the arm. Pushing on the bag with an elbow forces air through a set of reeds in a pipe called the *chanter.* The piper plays different notes by covering and uncovering holes in the chanter with his or her fingers.

Brass Instruments Brass instruments are also wind instruments, played by blowing. But they are made of brass or other metal, and they do not have reeds. The player produces sounds by blowing into a metal mouthpiece in a way that makes the lips vibrate. The vibrations are carried through a long tube and come out at the *bell* —the wider end of the tube. If you are looking at an orchestra or band, you can usually see the round, shiny bells of some of the brass instruments pointed at the audience.

The players change pitches by tensing or relaxing the lips. Most brass instruments also have three *valves*, buttons that the player can push to change the pitch of the notes.

The largest brass instrument—and the one with the lowest voice—is the *tuba*. Its cousin, the *sousaphone,* wraps all around the player and rests on one shoulder. Sousaphones are used in marching bands and some concert bands. Tubas can be used in concert bands or orchestras.

Brass instruments: trombone (top left), French horn (top right), tuba (below right), and trumpet (bottom).

The *trombone* and *baritone horn* have slightly higher voices. The baritone horn looks like a smaller brother of a tuba and has valves to change pitch. The trombone has no valves to change pitch. Instead, it has a slide. The player can change the pitch of the trombone's sound by moving the slide back and forth. If the slide is pushed out, the sound gets lower. If it is pulled in, the sound gets higher.

The brass instrument with the next highest voice is the *French horn.* Its tubing is rolled up into a circle, with the bell pointing backward. The player plays it with one hand on the valves and the other in the bell. French horns have a pleasing, mellow sound and are used in symphony orchestras.

The highest-voiced brass instruments are the *trumpet* and *cornet.* They are very much alike, but the trumpet is slightly larger and has a richer sound.

One brass instrument with a special use is the *bugle.* It looks like a cornet or trumpet, but it has no valves. Because it has no valves, it usually plays only five notes. Bugle calls are used in the armed forces to wake people up, signal time for bed, and give signals on the battlefield. The most familiar bugle call is *taps,* played at the end of the day and at a soldier's funeral.

Stringed Instruments Instruments in this family all have tightly stretched strings made of animal intestines, plastic, or metal. A player makes a musical sound by plucking a string with a finger or *pick*—a small piece of plastic or metal—or by drawing a wood and horsehair *bow* across the string. The player changes the strings' pitches by making them shorter or longer. The player usually does this by pressing the strings down with his or her fingers.

The string family is the most important family in the symphony orchestra. In most orchestras, more than half the players are playing stringed instruments. The four kinds of stringed instruments used in an orchestra look very much the same except for their size.

The smallest of the string family is the *violin*. A player tucks one end of the violin—the soundboard—under his or her chin and holds the other end—the *neck*—with the left hand. Four strings stretch along the *fingerboard*. By pressing the strings with the fingers of the left hand, the player changes pitches. With the right hand, the player draws a bow across the strings, making the sound. In many pieces for orchestra, the violins play the melody.

The *viola* is slightly larger than the violin and is held in the same way. It has somewhat lower voice and a nice, rich tone.

The *cello* looks like a giant violin. The player sits on a chair and holds the cello between his or her legs. A pin coming out of the bottom of the soundboard rests on the floor. The neck is in the player's left hand, and the bow is in the right hand. The cello plays notes lower than the violin or the viola.

The *string bass*, or *double bass*, is about twice as tall as the cello, standing about 6 feet (1.8 meters). Players stand to play the string bass, or sit on a high stool. The string bass has the lowest voice of all the strings. It is an important rhythm instrument in many jazz bands. (*See* **jazz.**)

Stringed instruments (left to right): violin, viola, string bass, and cello.

There are many other stringed instruments. The *harp* stands as high as a string bass and has more than 70 strings. Each string is a different length and so has a different pitch. The player plucks the strings with the fingers of both hands. A harp is sometimes used in a symphony orchestra.

One of the oldest stringed instruments is the *guitar*. Most guitars have six strings. The player holds the instrument across his or her body, fingering the strings with the left hand and plucking them with the right hand. Other stringed instruments include *dulcimers, mandolins,* and *lutes.*

Some instruments, such as the piano, have strings but are played on a keyboard. These instruments are placed in a separate family—keyboard instruments.

Percussion Instruments Another large family of instruments is the percussion family. Percussion instruments are played by hitting. The word *percussion* comes from a Latin word meaning "to hit."

The most familiar percussion instruments are the drums. In a symphony orchestra, there is a set of *kettle drums* called *timpani*—the largest of all the drums. A timpani player stands behind two, three, or four of these huge, kettle-shaped drums. A skin is tightly stretched over the top of each drum. When the player strikes the skin, the drum produces a deep, hollow *boom*. A pedal under each drum allows the player to change the pitch of the drums. Most other drums have only one pitch.

Another familiar kind of drum is the *bass drum*. It, too, is a large drum. But it can be carried. You will often see it in a marching band. Its big *boom* helps marchers keep in step.

The marching band usually has *snare drums* as well. They are smaller and are played with wooden drumsticks. When the top skin is hit, wires stretched tightly across the bottom vibrate. This gives these drums their familiar "sssss" sound.

The steel drum is a percussion instrument that can play melodies and harmony. A steel drum is a rounded piece of sheet metal. A skilled player uses two mallets to get ringing sounds from the steel drum. Steel bands using these steel drums are popular in the West Indies.

Another group of percussion instruments makes bell-like sounds. The *triangle* is one of these. Another, the *xylophone,* is made of wooden bars arranged in a row from high pitch to low. The xylophone player can play a tune by striking the bars with short sticks called *mallets.*

Many percussion instruments are not in any particular group. Each has a special sound. The *tambourine* has skin stretched over a round frame. It also has loose metal parts that jangle. *Maracas* are gourds or gourd shapes filled with small pebbles or beans. The player shakes them like a baby's rattle. They are used in South American and Caribbean music. *Castanets* are pairs of slightly scooped out wooden disks. A pair is held in one hand and sharply clicked together. Castanets give rhythm to Spanish

Percussion instruments are those that the player hits or shakes.

dances. A *cymbal* is like a big brass dish. It can be hit with a wooden stick, or two cymbals can be clashed together. Some music calls for a wooden block to be hit with a hard wooden stick.

The piano is sometimes called a percussion instrument. When the player strikes the keys, hammers inside the piano hit some of the strings. In some jazz groups, the piano does work as a percussion instrument. See more about the piano in the section on keyboard instruments, below.

Keyboard Instruments   A fifth family of instruments are those with keyboards. A keyboard instrument has a row of keys. On pianos and organs, the keys are black and white. Each key, when pressed, produces a note with its own pitch.

One of the earliest keyboard instruments is the *pipe organ.* Organs were built in churches in Europe beginning in the 900s. Today, many churches around the world have organs. In the 1920s, special theater organs were built to provide music during silent movies.

In some ways, a pipe organ is a woodwind instrument. When a player presses a key, air blows through one of hundreds of pipes in the organ, making a sound. There must be at least one pipe for each pitch on the organ.

Keyboard instruments range from
a giant pipe organ (above)
to an accordion (above right)
and an electronic synthesizer (right).

On large organs, there may be several pipes with the same pitch, each with a different tone color. An organ may have two or even three keyboards, so the player can play in several different voices at once.

Other keyboard instruments have strings instead of pipes. The most familiar is the *piano.* When you press a key on a piano, the key pushes a hammer. The hammer hits a string inside the piano, making the sound. (*See* **piano.**)

Before the piano was invented, a keyboard instrument called the *harpsicord* was popular. In a harpsicord, pushing a key causes a string to be plucked. That is why a harpsicord sounds a little like a guitar, even though it looks very much like a piano.

Another instrument with a keyboard is the *accordion.* It is also a kind of woodwind. When the player squeezes the accordion and then stretches it out again, wind rushes through reeds in the accordion. The player

presses keys on a keyboard to play particular notes.

Electronic Instruments Since the 1920s, electricity and electronics have brought many changes to music.

The first step was to change musical sounds into electric messages so the music could be *amplified*—made louder. When the strings of a guitar were connected to an electric amplifier, a new instrument, the *electric guitar,* was created. Rock groups use electric guitars and other electrified instruments.

Engineers found ways to make sound through electronics. One of their first successes was an *electronic organ.* Many people have electronic organs in their homes. Others hear such organs in churches.

The engineers studied the sounds of musical instruments very carefully. They found ways to describe the sound of a flute or a cello by using mathematics. In the 1960s, musical computers began to imitate the sounds of individual instruments and even small orchestras. Gradually, engineers developed a new musical machine called the *synthesizer*. A synthesizer can make the sounds of many instruments. It can also make musical sounds that no traditional instrument can make. Musicians learn to "play" the synthesizer. Performers use synthesizers in live performances and for studio recordings.

See also **band** and **orchestra**.

musical terms

Learning to read music is a lot like learning a new language. The language of music uses special terms—symbols and words. Musicians all over the world use the same musical terms. Even musicians who speak different languages can play music together, because they all understand the same musical language.

Musical Notation The symbols we use for writing a musical piece or song are called *musical notation*. Musical notation begins with a *staff*—five straight horizontal lines. The lines and spaces between them stand for *pitch*—whether the sound is high or low. On the staff, we place rounded *notes*, one for each sound a voice or a musical instrument makes. A note's position on the staff shows its pitch. The higher the note is placed on the staff, the higher the pitch. Pitches are named by letters of the alphabet, from *A* through *G*.

The notes shown on this staff show the pitches going up from *middle C*. On a piano, middle *C* is in the middle of the keyboard, and all the notes shown here are white keys.

There are two symbols that change the pitch—the *sharp* and the *flat*. When a sharp symbol is placed before a note, it means the pitch is slightly sharper—higher—than that shown on the staff. For example, a *D*-note with a sharp represents the black key on the piano between *D* and *E*.

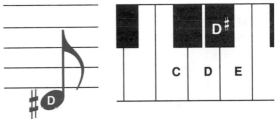

D-sharp is half a step higher in pitch than *D*.

The flat symbol in front of a note means the note is played slightly flatter—lower—than shown. A *D*-flat represents the black key on the piano between *D* and *C*.

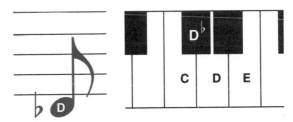

D-flat is half a step lower in pitch than *D*.

To show all the possible notes for instruments that play very high and very low, there must be more than one *clef*. A clef is a symbol at the beginning of a staff. A clef shows the range of pitches represented by

A note in musical notation is a symbol for a particular pitch. Below are middle *C* in notation and on a piano keyboard. The next highest note is *D*, and so on.

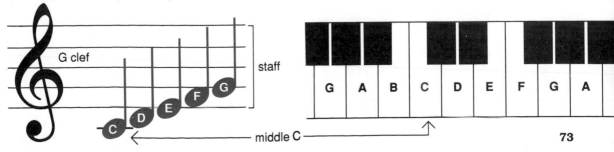

The names of the notes in the treble clef (left) and bass clef (right) are shown above. Those in the spaces in the treble clef spell the word *FACE*.

the staff. The *treble* clef shows that the staff lines represent pitches E, G, B, D, and F. The spaces represent pitches F, A, C, and E. The *bass* clef shows that the staff lines represent pitches G, B, D, F, and A. The spaces represent pitches A, C, E, and G. Both clefs are used in piano music. For most other instruments, one clef or the other is used.

Pieces of music are written in musical *keys*. Musical notation tells you the key by placing the flat or sharp symbols on certain lines or spaces right after the clef sign at the beginning of each staff. As you play the piece, all notes that fall on these lines or spaces are played sharp or flat. The key of *C* has no sharps or flats. The key of *G* has one sharp—*F*-sharp.

Another part of musical notation is rhythm. Look at the notes below. The difference in the way they look tells a musician how long to play each one. A *whole note* is usually held a long time. A *half note* is held half as long as a whole note. In the time it takes to play a whole note, you can play 4 *quarter notes*. You could also play 8 *eighth notes*, 16 *sixteenth notes*, and so on.

The *time signature* also tells something about rhythm. The time signature is found at the beginning of the piece. It shows two numbers, one written below the other. The number on the bottom tells what kind of note gets one beat. For example, if the bottom number is 4, a quarter note gets one beat. If the bottom number is 8, an eighth note gets one beat.

The top number in the time signature tells how many beats there are in one *measure* of music. A measure is a short section of the music. On the staff, measures are marked off by vertical lines called *bar lines*. If the top number is a 3, there are three beats in each measure. This often means that the first beat is strongest. The rhythm of the music will be "ONE-two-three, ONE-two-three." Waltzes and minuets are two kinds of dance music that have three beats to the measure.

Musical Words Besides using rounded notes, lines, numbers, and other symbols, musical notation also uses words. Most of the words come from the Italian language, because many great early musicians were Italians. Musicians from other countries often studied in Italy.

Some musical words are used for *tempo markings*. The tempo marking tells the speed and mood of a musical piece. It appears at the beginning of a piece, just above the clef sign and time signature. The table below gives some of these words and their meanings.

In 4/4 time, a whole note gets four counts, a half note two counts, a quarter note one count, an eighth note half a count, and a sixteenth note a quarter of a count.

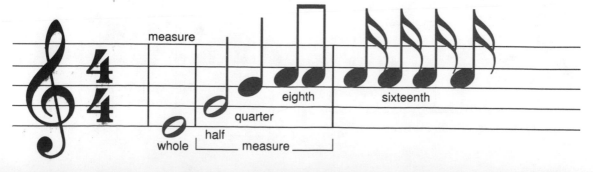

TEMPO

Word	Meaning
presto	as quickly as possible
allegro	quickly
allegretto	somewhat quickly
vivace	"with life," quickly
moderato	at medium speed
andante	at walking speed, medium
adagio	slowly
largo	very slowly

Some pieces are named for their tempo markings. *Adagio for Strings* is a beautiful, slow piece for string orchestra by the American composer Samuel Barber.

The tempo—speed—of many pieces changes from time to time. If there is a big change, there may be a new tempo marking. For smaller changes, directions are written below the musical staff. Three of the most common instructions are shown below.

CHANGE IN TEMPO

Abbrev.	Full Word	Meaning
rit.	ritardando	slow down gradually
accel.	accelerando	speed up gradually
	a tempo	go back to the original speed

Music can be marked to show how loudly or softly the musician should play. The table below shows some of these markings.

LOUDNESS

Abbrev.	Full Word	Meaning
ff	fortissimo	very loudly
f	forte	loudly
mf	mezzo forte	moderately loudly
mp	mezzo piano	moderately softly
p	p i a n o	softly
pp	pianissimo	very softly

When the music is to grow gradually louder or softer, this may be shown by a symbol, a word, or an abbreviation.

CHANGE IN LOUDNESS

Symbol, Abbrev.	Full Word	Meaning
◁ , **cresc.**	crescendo	play gradually louder
▷ , **dim.**	diminuendo	play gradually softer

Other Musical Terms There are many other musical terms and symbols. Some are used on all kinds of music. Others are used only in music for a particular instrument. For example, music for the violin may show *bowing marks* telling the violinist when to move the bow up or down. Piano music may include *fingering,* suggesting to the pianist which fingers to use for particular notes.

The best way to learn the language of musical terms is to learn to play music. The more you play, the more often you will come upon the different musical symbols and terms. Soon you will know what they mean without having to "translate" them.

See also **music; melody; rhythm; harmony;** and **musical instrument.**

Muslims, *see* Islam

mussel, *see* clams and mussels

mystery

A mystery is a story in which there is a puzzle. Often, the puzzle involves a crime, or it may be about a spy. There are books, movies, and television shows about mysteries. A mystery story is sometimes called a *whodunit*—who done it. You read the book or watch the show to find out who committed the crime and why they did it.

In a mystery story, there is always someone trying to solve the puzzle. This person is often a *detective*—someone hired to find a missing person or discover how a crime happened and who did it. The detective talks to people who may know something about the puzzle. If a crime was committed, the detective visits the place where it happened. The detective must have a keen eye and ear for details, and a good memory. Anything the detective sees or hears might be a *clue* —something that explains the puzzle. If the clues do not fit together, the detective finds out why.

People enjoy reading and watching mystery stories. They enjoy wondering what will happen next. They enjoy spotting clues and putting the pieces of the puzzle together. They enjoy guessing who is telling the truth and who is not. Often, one person in the story seems guilty at first. As the story continues, another person begins to look guilty. In the end, the solution often comes as a surprise. But thinking back over the clues, you can see how the solution makes sense.

Edgar Allan Poe is called the "father of the detective story." His story "The Murders in the Rue Morgue," printed in 1841, is considered the first modern crime mystery. Since then, there have been many well-known mystery writers. Their detectives have become popular through books, movies, and television and radio shows. Sir Arthur Conan Doyle invented the famous detective Sherlock Holmes in 1887. Mysteries by Agatha Christie have been made into movies and television shows. Perry Mason, created by Erle Stanley Gardner, has appeared in books, and on radio and television. Perry Mason is a lawyer whose work often involves solving mysteries. Mike Hammer is a popular television detective. One of the best-loved detectives of books and movies is Sam Spade—created by Dashiell Hammett. Raymond Chandler's detective Philip Marlowe is also famous.

Encyclopedia Brown is a boy detective featured in Donald Sobol's series of mystery books. Other mysteries for young readers are the Nancy Drew and Hardy Boys series.

See also **Holmes, Sherlock; American writers;** and **children's books.**

mythical creatures

Monsters and other imaginary creatures appear in many myths. These creatures are often a patchwork of animal and human bodies. They have unusual strength and powers. Some are helpful to people. Others are fierce and dangerous.

Greek myths tell of the fire-breathing Chimera, which had a lion's head and claws, a goat's shaggy body, and a snake's tail. It

The Chimera is a monster with the heads of a lion and a goat, and a snake for a tail. In Greek myth, a hero kills the Chimera with the help of Pegasus, the winged horse.

A mermaid has the upper body of a woman and the lower body of a fish.

frightened the people of Lycia, part of Greece. Today, we call a fantasy or an impossible dream a *chimera.*

Pegasus was a mythical winged horse that helped the Greek hero Bellerophon defeat the Chimera. Pegasus flew above the monster so Bellerophon could aim arrows down at it.

The Sphinx had a lion's body, a woman's head, and a pair of large wings. It sat on a rock over a road leading to the ancient Greek city of Thebes. According to many stories, the Sphinx stopped travelers and asked them a riddle. If they could not answer, the Sphinx ate them. The riddle was "What creature goes on four legs in the morning, two in the afternoon, and three at night?" The answer is "Man." A person crawls on four legs as a baby, stands on two legs during the prime of life, and uses a cane in old age.

Not all mythical creatures are monsters. The phoenix was a beautiful golden bird. It would live for 500 years, then set itself on fire. The fire brought the bird back to life all over again. We still speak of people and things as rising from the ashes "like a phoenix." We mean they have come back with renewed strength.

The unicorn is a creature that appears in legends from medieval Europe. The unicorn has the body and head of a horse, the legs of a deer, the tail of a lion, and a horn in the middle of its forehead. The unicorn was supposed to be shy and hard to catch. It became tame only in the presence of an unmarried woman. The unicorn is a symbol of purity and gentleness.

According to European folklore, mermaids are creatures that live in the sea. From the waist up, a mermaid has the body of a woman. From the waist down, it has the body of a fish. Beautiful mermaids are often pictured sitting on rocks, combing their long hair. Stories have been told of sailors who drowned trying to follow them to the bottom of the ocean.

Bigfoot is an American mythical beast—a giant ape-man. Some people believe it actually exists, hiding in the mountains and woods of North America. Another mythical ape-man is the Yeti, also called the Abominable Snowman. It is said to live in the Himalaya Mountains of Tibet.

See also **dragon** and **myths and legends.**

In Greek myth, Pegasus is a horse that has wings and can fly.

myths and legends

Myths and legends are two kinds of stories. They both tell about unusual, often magical, characters and events. But myths and legends are not the same. Myths are stories about gods and goddesses of some long-ago time. Myths were originally sacred stories. Legends may be about real people and events or imaginary people and events. Legends always take place during actual periods of history. They may be about heroes with superhuman abilities, but they are not religious stories.

Myths Since myths were sacred stories, they often supplied answers to basic questions that people have always asked about life and nature. Myths have been told that explain how the world and the first people were created, why there is good and evil in the world, and why there is death.

The best way to understand a myth is to read an example of one. Below is a Greek myth explaining how there came to be the passage of the seasons through the year. The Greeks were very moved by this story. They even had religious rituals that were based on Demeter's search for her missing child, Persephone. These were called the Eleusinian mysteries.

Persephone was a mythical character, not a real person. The story takes place at an unknown time very long ago, before the seasons began.

GREEK MYTHS

Persephone and Demeter

There was once a beautiful girl named Persephone. She loved to play in a field of flowers not far from where she lived with her mother, Demeter. Demeter was the goddess of grains and other growing things. One day Hades, the god of the underworld, saw Persephone and fell in love with her. He kidnapped the girl and brought her to his kingdom of the dead to be his bride.

As soon as Demeter realized her daughter was missing, she began to mourn. Her grief was so great that she refused to allow any plants to grow. Soon, all the earth's animals and people were starving.

Zeus, the king of the heavens, knew he had to do something to set things right again. He told Demeter that she could bring her daughter back from the underworld if the girl had not eaten there. Demeter agreed.

Unfortunately, Persephone did not know about the agreement. She nibbled on a few pomegranate seeds. As a result, Hades refused to let her leave. But Demeter was just as stubborn as Hades. She insisted that if her daughter was not returned, nothing would ever grow on the earth again.

Zeus suggested a compromise — that Persephone would live for three-quarters of the year with her mother, and one-quarter of the year with her husband. Everyone agreed with this plan. That is why fruits, flowers, and other plants grow on the earth for three seasons — spring, summer, and fall. During these seasons, Persephone is with her mother, playing in the fields. But in the winter, Persephone must go to the underworld with her husband. Then Demeter mourns the loss of her child and allows nothing to grow until the girl returns in the spring.

Persephone

Pandora

Pandora was the first woman on Earth. All the gods gave her gifts, such as beauty and love of music. The name Pandora means "all gifts." She was also given a beautiful gold box. Inside it, the gods placed all the evils and sins of the world. They did put one good thing in the box, and that was hope. The gods told Pandora that she must never open the golden box. One day, she opened it anyway, and all the evils came out in an ugly brown cloud. She closed the box just in time to keep hope from escaping.

Pygmalion and Galatea

Pygmalion was king of Cyprus and a talented sculptor. He could never find a woman worthy of becoming his queen. He carved a life-size ivory statue of a woman. The statue was so beautiful that he fell in love with it. Pygmalion asked Aphrodite, the goddess of love, to help him find a woman as perfect as his statue. Instead, Aphrodite turned the statue into a living woman, named Galatea. Pygmalion was very grateful. He married Galatea, and they had a son named Paphos.

Theseus

Theseus was the son of Aegeus, the king of Athens. Each year, Athens was forced to send children to Crete to be fed to the Minotaur, a monster with the body of a man and the head of a bull. Theseus sailed to Crete to kill the Minotaur in a ship with black sails. He said that if he killed the Minotaur, he would return with white sails on his ship. Theseus killed the Minotaur, but he sailed into Athens without changing his sails. Thinking Theseus had died, Aegeus killed himself, and Theseus became king.

Daedalus and Icarus

Daedalus was a craftsman on the island of Crete. After Theseus killed the Minotaur, Daedalus helped him escape. The king of Crete put Daedalus and his son Icarus in prison. They escaped from prison, but had no way to leave the island. Daedalus used wax and thread to make bird feathers into wings. Father and son flew away from Crete. Icarus loved flying so much that he flew high into the air. The wax on his wings melted, and the feathers fell off. Icarus fell into the sea and drowned.

Pandora

Pygmalion and Galatea

Theseus and the Minotaur

Icarus

Legends Legends, on the other hand, are often partly true. They are set in familiar time periods. For example, we do not know who the real King Arthur was, but some people believe he was a chief in Wales in the 400s. There may also have been a lumberjack named Paul Bunyan working in the American Northwest in the 1800s. He may have been especially strong, but certainly not as big or powerful as legends say he was. The legendary Paul Bunyan could pull the twists and turns out of rivers with the help of his giant ox, Babe. Real lumberjacks probably wished someone could straighten the rivers so the logs would float down without jamming together.

According to legend, Pecos Bill fell out of his family's covered wagon while they were crossing the Pecos River. He was just a baby and was rescued and raised by wolves. This legendary American cowboy is said to have later lassoed a tornado. More than one American cowboy living in the 1800s lost his family as a baby. But it is unlikely that any were raised by wolves—and lassoing a tornado is clearly impossible.

Stories about Robin Hood and his men and King Arthur and his knights are legends, not myths. They all take place in real places and times. Robin Hood's band is said to have camped in England's Sherwood Forest in the Middle Ages. King Arthur had his court at Camelot in the Dark Ages. Although no one knows exactly where Camelot was, it was supposed to be in England. Stories about the Trojan War are partly legend and partly myth. The war actually took place—in Hissarlik, in Turkey, in 1300 B.C. But some of the characters in the stories are mythical Greek gods and goddesses.

Davy Crockett, Daniel Boone, and George Washington are some of the real people in history who have become legendary. George Washington was certainly a real man who lived from 1732 to 1799. He was the first president of the United States. But we do not know for sure if he ever chopped down his father's cherry tree, then admitted it, saying, "I cannot tell a lie."

Davy Crockett was a person who lived from 1786 to 1836. He was born in Tennessee, was a member of the U.S. Congress, and died at the Alamo in Texas. But many legends about this rugged frontiersman may not be entirely true. The story about his tamed bear is one example.

See also **gods and goddesses; mythical creatures; Arthur, King; Bunyan, Paul; Henry, John; Pecos Bill; Robin Hood; tall tale;** and **Trojan War.**

AN AMERICAN LEGEND

Davy Crockett's Tamed Bear

They say Davy Crockett was such a good bear-hunter that he once tamed a wild bear to sit in the cabin and smoke a pipe with him. Yep, and when Old Davy would come home after a long day of shooting, why that bear would be right there to open the door for him. He also churned butter for Davy's wife. But if Davy wanted anything, well that bear would just drop the butter churner and run to Crockett's side. You could tell he knew what side his bread was buttered on.

The oldest form of the letter *N* was the ancient Egyptian picture writing for "water."

Ancient Middle Eastern tribes used a similar symbol. They called this letter *nun*, meaning "fish."

When the Romans borrowed this letter from the Greeks, they wrote it like our capital *N*.

names

A name is the word or group of words by which a person is known. Places, ships, spacecraft, books, stories, and many other things have names, too. But here we will talk only about people's names.

Most people today have at least two names—a *given name* and a *family name*. The family name is sometimes called the *surname* or *last name*. Many people also have *middle names*. The customs of a country and of a family help determine a person's names.

Naming Customs In most countries of Europe and the Americas, the given name comes first and the family name comes last. In China and some other Asian countries, the family name comes first and the given name comes last. When people from these Asian countries move to America or Europe, they may change the order of their names.

In some countries, middle names are very important. In Russia, a person's middle name is the father's first name with a *suffix* —an added ending—that means "son of" or "daughter of." A friend is always greeted by both the first and middle names. In Chinese names, the middle name is a generation name. All cousins that belong to the same generation of a family have the same generation name.

In Spanish-speaking countries, the surname includes the father's and mother's surnames connected with *y*—"and." For example, Mexican patriot Miguel Hidalgo y Costilla's father's surname was Hidalgo and his mother's father's surname was Costilla.

NAMES AROUND THE WORLD

AMERICAN

Sharon	**Eugenia**	**Brown**
given name	middle name	father's family name

RUSSIAN

Aleksey	**Nicolayevich**	**Tolstoy**
given name	father's given name + "son of"	father's family name

SPANISH

Maria	**Marquez**	**Garcia**
given name	father's family name	mother's family name

A lake in Massachusetts once had this long name:

Chaugogagog-manchaugogagog-chabunagungamog

People said that the name meant: "You fish on your side, we fish on our side, nobody fishes in the middle."

In the United States, a woman may use her *maiden name*—the family name she was born with—as her middle name after she marries.

Some religions have rules or customs about naming babies. Catholics often pick saints' names for their babies. Many Christians use names from the Bible. Jewish families usually name a child for someone in the family who is no longer living.

American Indian tribes have their own traditional naming customs. Many Indian names have religious meaning, and many are drawn from nature. An Indian may be given one name at birth but take new names later in life. For example, back in the 1800s, there was a boy of the Sioux tribe called Hunkesni, which meant "Slow." But after showing his bravery as a warrior, the boy was given a new name, Tatanka Iyotake—"Sitting Bull." Sitting Bull became a great Sioux chief. (*See* **Sitting Bull.**)

Given Name The given name is sometimes called a *first name* or *forename.* Many Christians call it the *Christian name.* For thousands of years, people used only the one name.

Many English names come from Hebrew, Greek, Latin, or German words for things. For example, Robert means "bright fame." Dorothy means "gift of God." Margaret

means "pearl." Names such as Violet and Pearl, mean the same as the English words.

Family Names Many family names began as names meaning "son of." John Robertson was John the son of Robert. *Mac* or *Mc* at the beginning of Scottish and Irish names means "son of." The *O'* at the beginning of some Irish names, *ben* at the beginning of Hebrew names, and *ibn* before Arab names also mean "son of."

Some family names, such as Baker and Miller, came from what people did for a living. Other names told where people lived. A person living near a woods might be Atwood. Someone living in Surrey might get Surrey as a last name. People might be named for their appearance or character. A short person might have been named Small.

Some family names change over time. Many were not written down, and people changed the ways they were pronounced. Members of a family who moved to another country might end up with different spellings of the same name. This happened to many people who moved to the United States in the early 1900s.

OLD FAMILY NAMES ONCE TOLD:

Who a person's father was:

Gustaf Gustaf*son*	= *son* of Gustaf (English, Scandinavian)
Ivan Ivan*ovich*	= *son* of Ivan (Russian)
Patrick *Fitz*gerald	= *son* of Gerald (Irish)
Kevin *Mc*Andrew	= *son* of Andrew

Where a person lived:

Ford	= by the ford in the river
Hill	= on the hill
Forest	= in the forest

What a person did:

Smith	= blacksmith
Carpenter	= carpenter
Cooper	= cooper (barrel maker)

"Ike" was the nickname of Dwight Eisenhower, who was twice elected president.

Names and Marriage In most countries, women and children take the husband's family name. Many women today choose to keep their maiden names. They do not use their husbands' names at all, or use both their maiden names and their husband's family name. A few men use their own names and their wives's maiden names.

Nicknames Nicknames are used instead of or in addition to real names. Many nicknames come from a first name. For example, Cathy and Kate are nicknames for Catherine. Nicknames for John are Jack and Johnny. People get nicknames from their last names, or because of a personal quality. President Dwight D. Eisenhower was sometimes called "Ike." Edward Kennedy Ellington was called "Duke" because he had a noble manner.

Name Changing Some people choose to change their names. They may change their names legally, or use a made-up name when they do certain work. Many writers sign their work with *pen names*. Samuel Clemens used the pen name Mark Twain. Pen names are also called *pseudonyms*—false names. Many performers use *stage names* instead of their real ones.

Names are important to people. When naming children, most parents try to think of names that sound good together.

Namibia, *see* Africa

Napoleon

Napoleon was a ruler of France and a great military leader. He conquered much of Europe in the early 1800s. He ruled France for 15 years, bringing changes that still affect French life. Napoleon was a man of energy and daring. But his ambition drove him too far, and he was eventually defeated.

Napoleon Bonaparte was born in 1769 on the island of Corsica, in the Mediterranean Sea. As a youth, he went to military school. There he was nicknamed the "Little Corporal" because he was short.

Napoleon joined the French army in 1786. In 1789, the French Revolution broke out. Napoleon fought with the revolutionary forces. France also became involved in wars with its neighbors. Napoleon went to Italy to fight the Austrians. After defeating them, he took an army to the Middle East and fought the Turks and the British. He was a skilled military leader, relying on speed and boldness. His soldiers loved him because he inspired them with confidence.

Napoleon seized power and became the ruler of France in 1799. In 1804, he crowned himself emperor of France and crowned his wife, Josephine, empress. Napoleon was a strong ruler. He reorganized the school system, set up the Bank of France, and changed the nation's taxes and money. He also formed a new system of laws, called the *Napoleonic Code.*

Meanwhile, France was still at war with its neighbors. French armies invaded Spain, Italy, Belgium, the Netherlands, and Germany. Napoleon replaced many rulers with his relatives and friends.

Napoleon made his first big mistake in 1812, when he invaded Russia with an army of 600,000 men. The Russians retreated,

Napoleon conquered most of Europe, but his rule lasted only a few years.

drawing the French deeper and deeper into their vast country. Napoleon reached Moscow, but the Russians had burned their own city and left it empty. Napoleon decided to go back. By then, winter had set in. The French forces were defeated by cold and hunger. Only 100,000 men escaped from Russia.

Napoleon's enemies now joined together and defeated him in 1814. He was sent away to live on the island of Elba in the Mediterranean. A year later, he escaped to Paris. Again he took power and gathered an army. But in 1815, Napoleon was defeated for good, at Waterloo, in Belgium. He was then sent far away to Saint Helena, an island in the south Atlantic Ocean. He died there in 1821.

narcotics, *see* drugs and medicines; addiction

nation, *see* country

Nation, Carry

"Men, I have come to save you from a drunkard's fate!" A hundred years ago, these words would have meant that Carry Nation had arrived. She often used a hatchet to destroy saloons and smash their bottles of liquor.

Carry Amelia Moore was born in 1846 in Garrard Country, Kentucky. Her hatred of alcohol began at age 21, when she married Dr. Charles Gloyd. For two years, she watched her husband drink himself to death.

Then she met and married a minister, David Nation. She came to believe that God wanted her to end the drinking of alcohol in the United States. She even believed that her name was a sign—Carry A. Nation.

The Nations lived in Kansas, which had laws against the sale of alcohol. But the laws were often disobeyed, and there were plenty of saloons. This breaking of the law enraged Carry Nation. She was fierce and frightening when angry. She stood almost 6 feet (1.8 meters) tall and weighed 175 pounds (79

For more than 50 years, Carry Nation crusaded against the sale of alcohol.

kilograms). Carry Nation and her hatchet did a lot of damage when she marched into a saloon. She was arrested for these violent actions, but she went right on, even in states that permitted alcohol.

Carry Nation died in 1911, after giving a lecture on the evils of alcohol. The United States did ban liquor, in 1919. But the ban was lifted just a few years later.

national park

A national park is a special area set aside for people to enjoy. National parks are maintained by the federal government. There are over 300 of these parks in the United States. Every state except Delaware has at least one.

There are four main kinds of national parks. One kind is noted for its beautiful or unusual natural features. Yellowstone National Park—the first national park in the world—is a park of this type. Others include Grand Canyon, Lassen Volcanic, and Mammoth Cave national parks, and Death Valley National Monument.

A second kind of national park is one that has been set aside for its historic interest. It may be a battlefield, such as Gettysburg National Military Park in Pennsylvania. It may be the home of a famous American, such as Thomas Edison's home in West Orange, New Jersey.

A third kind of national park is preserved as a recreation area. People use these parks for swimming, boating, fishing, hiking, and other outdoor activities. One such area is the Cape Cod National Seashore, in Massachusetts. Another is the Appalachian National Scenic Trail, which winds through the mountains from Georgia to Maine.

The fourth kind of national park is one that is devoted to the arts. One such park is the John F. Kennedy Center for the Performing Arts, in Washington, D.C.

See the Index for entries on individual national parks.

Glacier National Park in Montana (below left), Edison National Historic Site in New Jersey (below right), and Golden Gate National Recreation Area in California (above).

natural gas, *see* gas, natural

natural resources

Natural resources are the features or products of the earth that enable it to support life. The most basic natural resources are things you probably take for granted, such as air and sunshine. These are things that exist everywhere on Earth. Water, too, is a basic natural resource. Water comes as rain or snow and is stored in rivers, lakes, and oceans. Like air, water must be clean to support healthy living things. Another of our basic natural resources is soil. Some parts of the world have fertile soil—soil that has all the nutrients plants need to grow. Other parts of our planet are deserts or too rocky to support many plants.

Plants and animals are natural resources, too. Through the way they use the sun's energy, plants make possible all other life on earth. Plants need air, water, and fertile soil to produce the food humans and other animals need to eat. Plants also give us the oxygen we need to breathe. Animals supply us with food, wool, and leather. They perform other useful functions, too. For example, many insects pollinate plants, enabling the plants to reproduce.

Natural resources include all the minerals found on land and in the water. *Ores*—rocks and sand rich in minerals—are mined from the earth. Metals such as gold, silver, iron, lead, and tin come from ores. We rely on fuels that come from the earth—coal, oil, and natural gas.

One problem with natural resources is that they are not evenly spread over the earth. Some countries, such as the United States, have large supplies of almost every natural resource they need. Other countries do not, and if they cannot buy what they lack, their people suffer.

Another serious problem is that natural resources will not all last forever. For hundreds of years, humans have been helping

Soil, rain, and sunlight are natural resources important to raising food.

themselves to nature's gifts without much thought for the future. They have used poor farming methods and cut down forests, so that soil washed away. They have polluted the air and water.

Will we run out of basic resources? Some, called *renewable* resources, can be built up again. For example, good farming and conservation practices can restore the fertility of soil. But some resources are *nonrenewable*. For example, Earth has a limited supply of some minerals. Once we use them up, they are gone. To meet our future needs, we will have to conserve Earth's resources. We will have to do our best to renew some natural resources and find substitutes for others.

See also **conservation; ecology; environment;** and **energy.**

Nauru, *see* Pacific Islands

Navaho Indians, *see* Indians, American

navigation

In the days before modern electronic instruments, how did a ship's captain know what direction his ship was traveling in? If he was in sight of land, he could navigate—find his way—by judging his direction in relation to something visible on land. By sailing directly toward the landmark or directly away from it, he could navigate by *piloting.*

But what if the ship was out of sight of land? Then the captain might rely upon the sun. He would know that it rose in the east and set in the west. The sun could be helpful during the day when the weather was clear. But at night, the captain needed another guide. If he knew the stars and if the weather was clear enough for him to see them, he could use the stars.

For centuries, ship's captains needed to see land or the sun or the stars to be able to navigate. Then, around the year 1000, the compass was discovered. The compass pointed north all the time, even at night or in a storm. The compass changed the science of navigation completely. Columbus was able to travel all the way across the Atlantic by navigating with the help of a compass. (*See* **compass.**)

The next great aid to navigators, the *sextant,* was invented in 1731. The sextant was used to measure the angle between the horizon and the sun or stars. Once the navigator knew the exact location of the sun or another star, he could look up the ship's location in the nautical almanac, a book of tables. Along with better compasses and maps, sextants made navigation easier.

A captain could use another method, called *dead reckoning,* to find his location. If he knew his direction and speed, he could use a chart or map to make a good guess about where he was.

Today, we still use piloting and dead reckoning, with the help of instruments like compasses and sextants. We also have other ways of guiding ships—and aircraft—from place to place. By the 1930s, radio signals were used to improve navigation. Radar and sonar became important navigation aids in the 1940s. (*See* **radar and sonar.**)

Today, we use gyroscopic compasses, improved sextants, and more accurate maps for navigation. Satellites orbiting the earth give us even more navigation information. We have computers to calculate locations, destinations, and speeds. But navigators—even astronauts—still check this information by using their compasses or sextants and the sun and other stars. (*See* **gyroscope.**)

Navy, United States, *see* armed services

At left, a navigator plots a course through the sea in the navigation room of a ship. At right, radar helps air traffic controllers guide aircraft in for safe landings.

Nebraska

Capital: Lincoln
Area: 77,355 square miles (200,349 square kilometers) (15th-largest state)
Population (1980): 1,569,825 (1985): about 1,606,000 (36th-largest state)
Became a state: March 1, 1867 (37th state)

▲ Historical Sites and Points of Interest

Nebraska is a state in the center of the United States. The name *Nebraska* comes from an Indian word meaning "flat water." This was what the Indians called the Platte River. The Platte winds east through the middle of Nebraska for 400 miles (644 kilometers), on its way to the Missouri River. Early settlers used to say that the Platte was "a mile wide and an inch deep."

Land On a map, Nebraska is almost rectangular in shape. The wiggly eastern border follows the Missouri River.

Much of the state is made up of gently rolling, grass-covered prairie. Summers are hot and winters are cold. The wind blows most of the time.

Nebraska does not receive much rain, but it has a lot of underground water. This is used to irrigate farmlands. Nebraska's underground water and very rich soil have made it a great agricultural state. Corn is the chief crop. Wheat and other grains, soybeans, and hay are also important.

Early settlers in Nebraska found trees growing only on the banks of rivers. They missed the forests of their homelands so much that they began planting trees. Some were fruit trees. Others marked the boundaries of farms. Still others protected crops from the wind and helped keep the soil from blowing away. In the dry, sandy part of Nebraska—the Sand Hills—whole forests of evergreen trees were planted. The Nebraska

National Forest is the largest man-made forest area in the world. A man named J. Sterling Morton came up with the idea of having a special day each year when everyone would plant a tree. The idea caught on, and now Arbor Day is celebrated every April. (*See* **Arbor Day.**)

Western Nebraska has many large beef cattle ranches. The cattle are shipped to eastern Nebraska, where they are fattened with corn before going to market.

History Before the early 1800s, explorers, missionaries, and fur traders were almost the only white people in Nebraska. Spain, France, England, and various Indian tribes all claimed parts of it. The United States bought most of Nebraska in 1803, through the Louisiana Purchase. Shortly afterward, the first trading posts and forts were built. (*See* **Louisiana Purchase.**)

By the middle of the 1800s, several famous trails to the West crossed Nebraska. Great wagon trains of settlers and freight passed along the Mormon Trail, the Oregon Trail, and the California Trail. You can still see the marks of thousands of wagon wheels!

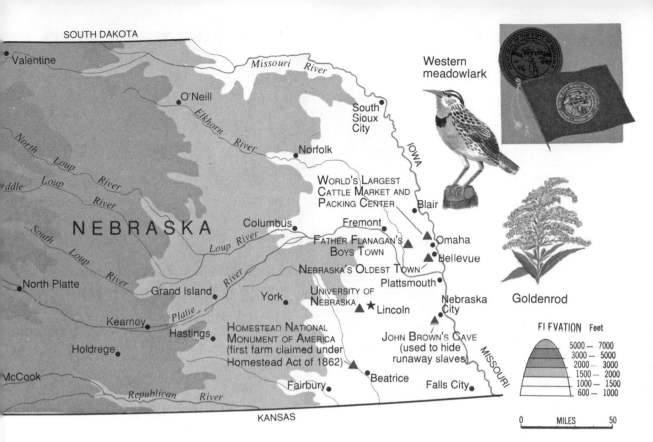

SOUTH DAKOTA

Valentine

Missouri River

O'Neill

South Sioux City

IOWA

Norfolk

Western meadowlark

Elkhorn River

North Loup River

Middle Loup River

NEBRASKA

WORLD'S LARGEST CATTLE MARKET AND PACKING CENTER

Blair

Columbus

Loup River

Fremont

FATHER FLANAGAN'S BOYS TOWN

Omaha

Bellevue

South Loup River

NEBRASKA'S OLDEST TOWN

Plattsmouth

North Platte

Grand Island

York

UNIVERSITY OF NEBRASKA

★ Lincoln

Nebraska City

Goldenrod

Kearney

Platte River

HOMESTEAD NATIONAL MONUMENT OF AMERICA (first farm claimed under Homestead Act of 1862)

JOHN BROWN'S CAVE (used to hide runaway slaves)

Hastings

Holdrege

MISSOURI

McCook

Fairbury

Beatrice

Falls City

ELEVATION Feet

Republican River

5000 — 7000
3000 — 5000
2000 — 3000
1500 — 2000
1000 — 1500
600 — 1000

KANSAS

0   MILES   50

In western Nebraska, the wagon trails led past Chimney Rock, a stone pillar that sticks up 500 feet (152 meters) above the plains. When the pioneers saw Chimney Rock, they knew they would soon begin the difficult passage through the Rocky Mountains. Many pioneers scratched their names into Chimney Rock.

Nebraska was opened up for settlement in 1854. Most people who came were either cattle ranchers or homesteaders. Under the Homestead Act, people received 160 acres of land, free, if they built a house, farmed the

A highway runs straight across the rich farmlands of Nebraska.

land, and lived there for five years. Ranchers and homesteaders did not always get along well with each other. But everyone had to struggle together. In some years, there were terrible blizzards, or no rain. Sometimes, masses of grasshoppers ate up every plant in sight.

People Today, most Nebraskans live in the eastern part of the state. The biggest city is Omaha, on the Missouri River. Omaha is the largest meat-packing center in the United States and the second-largest cattle market in the world. It is also the fourth-largest railroad center in the nation. The Omaha area is home to many insurance companies, too.

Many notable people have come from Nebraska. Among them are the actors Fred Astaire, Marlon Brando, and Henry Fonda. The writer Willa Cather, the black leader Malcolm X, and the television entertainer Johnny Carson also came from Nebraska.

In 1917, the Reverend Edward J. Flanagan founded Boys' Town near Omaha. It was one of the nation's first shelters for homeless boys. Boys' Town is a working farm. It is also a village, run entirely by the boys.

89

Negro history, *see* black Americans

neon

Neon is one of the elements. It is a colorless, odorless gas. It is called an *inert gas* or *noble gas* because, in nature, it does not combine with any other element. It becomes a liquid at -414° F (-248° C). Neon exists as a very small part of the air, yet it is the third-most-common element in the universe.

One kind of colored electric lights is often called "neon" lights. But these lights may not use neon at all. When an electric current passes through a glass tube filled with neon, the gas glows reddish orange. To get other colors, the glass tubes are filled with other gases. Argon gives a purple light. Krypton gives a pale violet color. Xenon glows light blue to green. A small amount of mercury added to the neon gives a blue color. "Neon" lights can be seen from a great distance. (*See* **lights and lighting.**)

Neon is used in some electronic instruments. For example, it is used in some television sets to control brightness.

Although no natural compounds of neon exist, scientists have successfully made some neon compounds by using special chemicals called *catalysts*. (*See* **compound.**)

Nepal, *see* Asia

Neptune

Neptune is the eighth planet out from the sun in our solar system. It is about 4.5 billion kilometers (3 billion miles) away from the sun and about 4.4 billion kilometers (2¾ billion miles) from Earth. Since Neptune is so far away, we know less about it than about any other planet except Pluto, which is even farther away most of the time.

Neptune's diameter—the distance in a straight line through its middle—is about

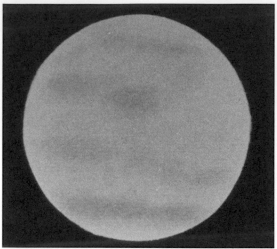

Neptune can scarcely be seen from Earth without a powerful telescope.

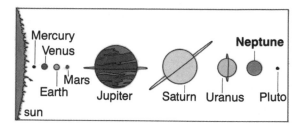

50,000 kilometers (31,000 miles). It is 4 times as big as Earth and 17 times heavier. Neptune has two small moons orbiting it.

Neptune is mainly a big ball of very cold gases. Its pale blue atmosphere is made up of hydrogen and helium, and does not support any life as we know it. In the part of the atmosphere where clouds form, the temperature is around -200° C (-328° F). Cold temperatures and pressure have probably turned the gases on Neptune's surface into either liquids or frozen solids.

A day on Neptune—the time it takes to make one rotation on its axis—lasts about 15½ hours. Because Neptune is so far from the sun, one orbit around the sun—one Neptune year—takes more than 164 Earth years.

See also **solar system.**

nerve

Nerves are cordlike fibers that link the body organs and muscles to the brain and spinal cord. Messages travel over nerves from every part of your body along the spinal cord in your back to the brain. In this way, the brain is kept informed of things going on inside and outside of the body. The brain processes this information and sends out messages through other nerves. These messages tell muscles and body organs how to respond. As a result, you walk, talk, laugh, cry, or otherwise behave as a human being.

Nerve Cells Nerves are made up of nerve cells. Like all other cells, nerve cells have a cell body and a nucleus. Unlike other cells, nerve cells have special threadlike parts, called *fibers,* extending from the cell body. Many short fibers—called *dendrites*—receive messages from other nerve cells and carry them to the cell body. A single, long fiber—the *axon*—carries messages away from the cell body to another nerve cell.

Nerve cells are so small that they can only be seen with a powerful microscope. But the nerve fibers are very long by comparison. If the cell body were enlarged to the size of a tennis ball, the fibers would fill a large room. In that enlargement, the fiber carrying messages away from the cell body could be up to a mile (1.6 kilometers) long, but only a half-inch (1.3 centimeters) wide.

The nerve fibers are bound together into nerves. Each nerve is a bundle of fibers. There may be thousands of fibers in a single nerve. They are like the wires in a telephone cable. Each nerve fiber is insulated from the others and acts by itself.

How Nerves Work Imagine that you are standing at a crosswalk. You stand and wait until the light turns green. When it does, you step off the curb and cross the street. Although this seems like a very simple action, there were actually many events that took place. When the light turned green, *color receptors* in your eyes picked up the message. The message was sent to the brain through nerve cells in the *optic nerves*—the nerves that connect the eyes to the brain.

A nerve impulse is something like an electric current. However, both chemical and electrical changes take place as a nerve

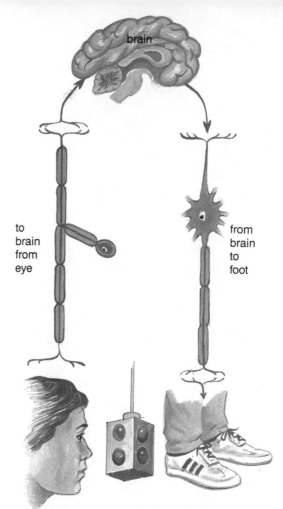

In a split second, nerves send signals from eye to brain ("light is green") and from brain to feet ("walk now").

impulse travels down a nerve cell. When the nerve impulse reaches the end of the nerve fiber, it causes the release of chemicals from the end of the nerve fiber. These chemicals move across a gap to the next nerve cell and cause it to become active.

When you see the green traffic light, the message "green light" travels through nerve cells until it reaches the brain. Some nerve cells in the brain translate the message, "The light is green." Other nerve cells in the brain change the message into a suggestion—"Walk across the street now." The brain sends messages out to the muscles. The messages travel along certain nerves as nerve impulses. When these messages reach the muscles, the muscles follow the orders given by the brain. Certain muscles contract and others relax. You walk across the street and safely reach the other side.

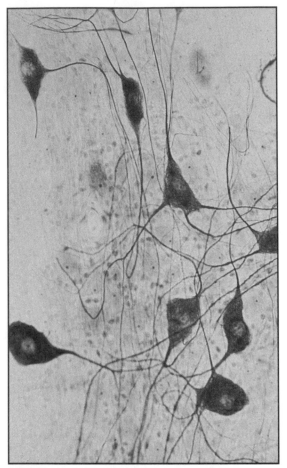

Highly magnified human nerve cells, connected to each other by thin axons.

Other Nerve Pathways Sometimes nerve impulses from the outer parts of the body do not travel all the way to the brain. Some impulses travel along special nerves to the spinal cord, and then back to the muscles. Think about what happens when you touch a hot object. Your hand pulls back at once. A message from nerves called *pain receptors* travels along nerves to the spinal cord. A new message travels back along nerves to the muscles in your hand. In response, your hand jerks away. The "pain" message also travels to the brain along other nerves. When it reaches the brain, you feel the pain. By this time, your hand is already safe. This reflex is a natural way that your body is protected. Some other human reflexes are coughing, sneezing, blinking, and jumping when frightened.

Some nerves control your body functions without your conscious control. These nerves connect all of the body's organs and glands to the spinal cord. These nerves tell the various organs to speed up or slow down. For example, think about what happens when you are hungry and smell food. Your mouth begins to water because a message is carried to your salivary glands. You are prepared to start eating. As you eat, messages travel to the stomach, intestines, liver, and other digestive organs telling them to start digesting the food.

Try to imagine what it would be like to live without nerves. You would not be able to sense anything about the outside world. Your internal organs would not work together as they should. Muscles would not be able to work together to move your body.

Fortunately, we all have nerves that connect the organs and muscles to the brain and spinal cord. Our brains can find out about the outside world, and our muscles and organs can respond properly.

See also **brain; spinal cord; muscle;** and **human body.**

Netherlands, The

Capital: Amsterdam
Area: 14,770 square miles (38,254 square kilometers)
Population (1985): about 14,481,000
Official language: Dutch

The Netherlands—also called Holland—is a country in northwestern Europe. *Netherlands* means "low country." Most of the country is near or below sea level. The people of the Netherlands are often called the Dutch.

The Netherlands is about twice the size of New Jersey and has about twice as many people. The country's farmlands are among the world's most productive. Dutch dairy farmers are especially famous for their cheeses. The Dutch ship flowers and bulbs, especially tulips, all over the world. Cheese and flower markets are a common sight in Dutch cities and towns. The Netherlands is also an important manufacturing country. Its factories make steel, ships, electronic equipment, and many other products.

Land and People The Netherlands has borders with West Germany, Belgium, and Luxembourg. The North Sea, on the west, is known for its fierce storms. For centuries, storms pushed seawater far into the lowlands, ruining crops and flooding towns. To protect their land, the people built *dikes* —seawalls—that hold back the water.

The Dutch learned to take land from the sea. They built dikes around large, shallow bays. Then they used windmills to pump out the water, turning the bays into fertile farmland. About one-fifth of the country's land was once underwater.

Water is important in the Netherlands in other ways. The Rhine River, one of the most important in Europe, branches out into the Netherlands. The city of Rotterdam, where

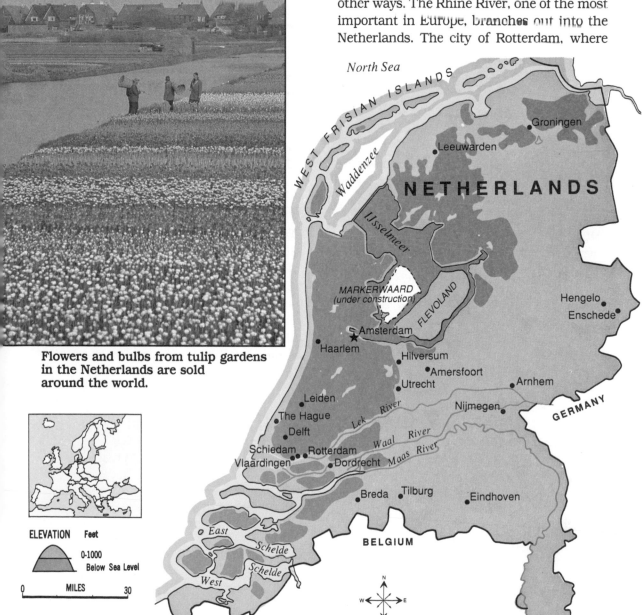

Flowers and bulbs from tulip gardens in the Netherlands are sold around the world.

ELEVATION   Feet

0-1000
Below Sea Level

0   MILES   30

the largest branch reaches the North Sea, is one of the world's biggest seaports. Many canals connect to the rivers. These canals are the "roads" on which farmers send their products to market.

Water has even played a role in the way people dress. Some people in the countryside still wear wooden shoes. These shoes give good protection against the damp ground.

History The Netherlands and its neighbors—Belgium and Luxembourg—have no mountains or seas to protect them from the rest of Europe. They have often been controlled by their powerful neighbors and have been battlegrounds in many wars.

In the 1100s, the region became an important area for shipbuilding, fishing, and trade. In the early 1500s, it was taken over by Spain. The Dutch did not like Spanish rule and were soon at war with Spain. They declared their independence in the 1580s, but battles continued for another 50 years.

During the 1600s, the Netherlands became one of the most powerful nations in Europe. The Dutch established colonies in many parts of the world. One, called New Amsterdam, was in North America. It included the present-day city of New York and the Hudson River valley. At home, Dutch artists became famous. The paintings of Rembrandt and Jan Vermeer can be seen in great museums all over the world.

The Netherlands did not stay so powerful, but its people were still good traders and travelers. Their country was peaceful and wealthy. The Dutch emigrated to many other parts of the world. Some—later called Afrikaaners—established a colony in South Africa. (*See* **South Africa.**)

Still, the Netherlands suffered when its neighbors went to war. In 1806, the French emperor Napoleon took over the country for a few years. In 1940, early in World War II, the Germans bombed Rotterdam and soon occupied all of the Netherlands. The Germans were defeated in 1945. The Dutch rebuilt Rotterdam and other damaged cities. (*See* **World War II.**)

Nevada

Capital: Carson City
Area: 110,561 square miles (286,353 square kilometers) (7th-largest state)
Population (1980): 800,508 (1985): about 936,000 (43rd-largest state)
Became a state: October 31, 1864 (36th state)

Nevada is a state in the western United States. The word *nevada* is a Spanish word meaning "snow-covered". That is a strange name for a desert state! It probably refers to the snow that covers the Sierra Nevada, mountains in the western part of the state.

Nevada is bordered by Oregon and Idaho on the north, and by California on the west. Utah and Arizona border Nevada on the east.

Land Nevada is in the part of the United States called the Great Basin. The Great Basin is between the Rocky Mountains to the east and the Sierra Nevada to the west. If you were looking down at Nevada from an airplane, you would see about 30 mountain ranges with broad, flat deserts between them. The mountains run north—south, with long, flat valleys between their ridges.

Nevada is the driest state in the United States. It receives only about 9 inches (23 centimeters) of rain every year. One reason for this is that it is in the "rain shadow" of the Sierra Nevada. The wind usually blows from the west. As it crosses the Pacific Ocean, it picks up moisture. When it hits the western slopes of the Sierra Nevada, in California, it is forced upward. The moisture condenses up high and falls as rain or snow. Little moisture is left to fall on Nevada.

Few trees grow in Nevada, except near rivers and lakes or up in the mountains. Cacti, sagebrush, and rabbitbrush grow in the desert. Many unusual animals live in the

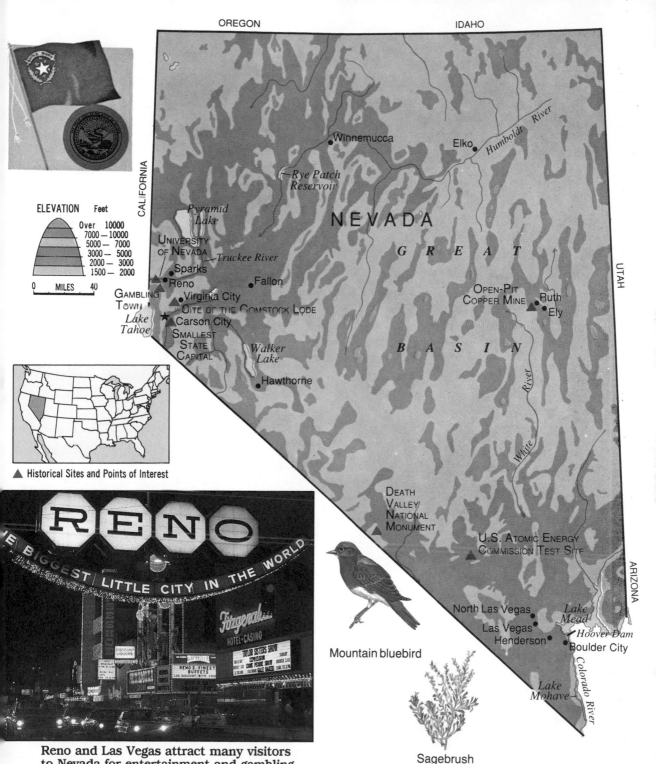

ELEVATION   Feet
Over 10000
7000 – 10000
5000 – 7000
3000 – 5000
2000 – 3000
1500 – 2000

0   MILES   40

▲ Historical Sites and Points of Interest

OREGON
IDAHO
CALIFORNIA
UTAH
ARIZONA

Winnemucca
Elko
Humboldt River
Rye Patch Reservoir
Pyramid Lake
NEVADA
GREAT
UNIVERSITY OF NEVADA
Truckee River
Sparks
Reno
Fallon
GAMBLING TOWN
Virginia City
OPEN-PIT COPPER MINE
Ruth
Ely
SITE OF THE COMSTOCK LODE
Lake Tahoe
Carson City
SMALLEST STATE CAPITAL
Walker Lake
BASIN
River
Hawthorne
White River
DEATH VALLEY NATIONAL MONUMENT
U.S. ATOMIC ENERGY COMMISSION TEST SITE
North Las Vegas
Lake Mead
Las Vegas
Henderson
Hoover Dam
Boulder City
Colorado River
Lake Mohave

Mountain bluebird

Sagebrush

Reno and Las Vegas attract many visitors to Nevada for entertainment and gambling.

desert. Roadrunners—birds of the cuckoo family—run over the sands on their powerful legs. Gila monsters—large, poisonous lizards—rest in the shade. Some of the mountains have strange shapes. One, which looks normal during the day, looks like a huge grinning skull at sundown!

History People have been living in Nevada for more than 20,000 years. When white men came to the area in the late 1700s, they found Navaho, Paiute, Shoshone, and "California group" Indians.

Early explorers claimed the land for Spain. Later, it belonged to Mexico, until the United

States won it in the Mexican War in 1848. The next year, the first permanent settlement was started by the Mormons, a religious group. They came from Utah in search of farmland.

Nevada became part of the Utah Territory in 1850. When gold and silver were discovered in the region, miners poured in. Nevada became a United States territory in 1861 and a state in 1864. Nevada is nicknamed the "Silver State." It is also known as the "Battle-Born State," because it was created during the Civil War. In fact, its gold and silver helped the North pay for the war.

For years, mining was the only important economic activity in Nevada. Wherever gold or silver was found, towns sprang up. Successful miners had nowhere to spend their money, so they set up their own saloons and gambling houses. When a mine was used up, the town near it was often abandoned. Now there are about 200 "ghost towns" in Nevada—about two out of every five towns in the state!

Agriculture began to be important in the early 1900s. The northern part of the state was used for cattle ranches. The dry desert was turned into farmland through irrigation. Dams were built across several rivers, creating reservoirs for storing water. The largest and most famous of these dams is Hoover Dam. It was built in 1936 across the

Colorado River, between the Nevada and Arizona border. (*See* **dam**.)

Lake Mead, the reservoir created by Hoover Dam, is a popular vacation resort. Lake Tahoe, near Reno and Carson City, is another important vacation spot.

Atomic weapons were tested in Nevada in 1951. The United States Air Force still has two bases in the state.

People Until the 1960s, there were fewer people per square mile in Nevada than in any other state. Between 1960 and 1970, the population doubled. Since then, it has almost doubled again.

About half of the people in Nevada live in or around Las Vegas, in the southeastern part of the state. Another quarter live in or near Reno, in west-central Nevada. The state capital is Carson City, one of the smallest state capitals in the United States. It was named after Kit Carson, who explored and mapped Nevada in the 1840s. Gambling has been legal in Nevada off and on for 120 years. The little saloons and gambling halls in dusty mining towns have been replaced by great, glittering casinos. Each year, about 15 million people come to the casinos in Las Vegas and Reno. In Las Vegas alone, they spend more than $1 billion a year. Visitors to Las Vegas and Reno can stay in fabulous hotels and watch world-famous entertainers perform in nightclubs.

Gambling and tourism are Nevada's main economic activities. More than a quarter of all Nevadans make their living from serving tourists who come to gamble or to vacation.

Mining is another major activity, but copper has become more important than gold and silver. Manufacturing does not play a large role in Nevada's economy, except for the processing of copper and other minerals. Agriculture is important, too. The chief crops are alfalfa, potatoes, hay, and barley. Farmers also raise cattle, sheep, hogs, and poultry.

The most unusual livestock in Nevada are ostriches. An ostrich race is held every year in the ghost town of Virginia City.

Lake Tahoe, high in the Sierra Nevada, is on the Nevada-California state line.